First World War
and Army of Occupation
War Diary
France, Belgium and Germany

46 DIVISION
139 Infantry Brigade
Sherwood Foresters
(Nottinghamshire and Derbyshire Regiment)
1/5 Battalion
1 March 1915 - 31 May 1919

WO95/2695/1

The Naval & Military Press Ltd
www.nmarchive.com
Published in association with The National Archives

Published by

The Naval & Military Press Ltd

Unit 10 Ridgewood Industrial Park,

Uckfield, East Sussex,

TN22 5QE England

Tel: +44 (0) 1825 749494

www.naval-military-press.com

www.nmarchive.com

This diary has been reprinted in facsimile from the original. Any imperfections are inevitably reproduced and the quality may fall short of modern type and cartographic standards.

© **Crown Copyright**
Images reproduced by permission of The National Archives, London, England, 2015.

Contents

Document type	Place/Title	Date From	Date To
Heading	WO95/2695 (1)		
Heading	46th Division 139th Infy Bde 5th Bn Notts & Derby Mar 1915-May 1919		
Heading	139th Inf. Bde. 46th Div. 5th Battn. The Sherwood Foresters (Nottinghamshire And Derbyshire Regiment). March 1915		
War Diary	Terdeghem	01/03/1915	04/03/1915
War Diary	Romarin	05/03/1915	09/03/1915
War Diary	Merris	10/03/1915	11/03/1915
War Diary	Bac St Maur	12/03/1915	13/03/1915
War Diary	Neuf Berquin.	14/03/1915	31/03/1915
War Diary	Havre	04/03/1915	06/03/1915
War Diary	Terdeghem	07/03/1915	11/03/1915
War Diary	139th Inf. 5Bde. 46th Div.5th Battn. The Sherwood Foresters (Nottinghamshire And Derbyshire Regiment). April 1915		
War Diary	Neuf Berquin	01/04/1915	03/04/1915
War Diary	Bailleul	04/04/1915	05/04/1915
War Diary	Locre	06/04/1915	09/04/1915
War Diary	Lindenhoek	10/04/1915	13/04/1915
War Diary	Locre	14/04/1915	17/04/1915
War Diary	Lindenhoek	18/04/1915	22/04/1915
War Diary	Locre	24/04/1915	27/04/1915
War Diary	Lindenhoek	28/04/1915	30/04/1915
Heading	139th Inf. Bde. 46th Div. 5th Battn. The Sherwood Foresters (Nottinghamshire And Derbyshire Regiment). May 1915		
War Diary	Locre	01/05/1915	05/05/1915
War Diary	Lindenhoek	06/05/1915	10/05/1915
War Diary	Locre	11/05/1915	13/05/1915
War Diary	Rossignol	14/05/1915	16/05/1915
War Diary	Little Kemmel	17/05/1915	20/05/1915
War Diary	Rossignol	21/05/1915	24/05/1915
War Diary	Little Kemmel	25/05/1915	29/05/1915
War Diary	Rossignol	30/05/1915	31/05/1915
Heading	139th Inf. Bde. 46th Div. 5th Battn. The Sherwood Foresters (Nottinghamshire And Derbyshire Regiment). June 1915		
Heading	War Diary of 1/5th Bn. Sherwood Foresters from 1st June 1915 to 30th June 1915		
War Diary	North of Kemmel	01/06/1915	02/06/1915
War Diary	Little Kemmel	03/06/1915	07/06/1915
War Diary	Trenches	08/06/1915	11/06/1915
War Diary	Little Kemmel	12/06/1915	15/06/1915
War Diary	Trenches	16/06/1915	19/06/1915
War Diary	Locre	20/06/1915	20/06/1915
War Diary	Vlamertinghe	21/06/1915	22/06/1915
War Diary	Zillebeke	23/06/1915	28/06/1915
War Diary	Poperinghe	29/06/1915	30/06/1915

Heading	139th Inf. Bde. 46th Div. 5th Battn. The Sherwood Foresters (Nottinghamshire And Derbyshire Regiment). July 1915		
Heading	War Diary of 1/5th Bn. the Sherwood Foresters. from 1st. July 1915 to 31st July 1915		
War Diary	Near Busseboom G 26. a. 1.9.	01/07/1915	11/07/1915
War Diary	Trenches around Sanctuary Wood	18/07/1915	18/07/1915
War Diary	Trenches	24/07/1915	25/07/1915
War Diary	Maple Copse	30/07/1915	30/07/1915
War Diary	Trenches	31/07/1915	31/07/1915
Heading	139th Inf. Bde. 46th Div. 5th Battn. The Sherwood Foresters (Nottinghamshire And Derbyshire Regiment). August 1915		
War Diary	In Trenches Around Sanltuary Wood about 1 mile $ of Hodge	01/08/1915	05/08/1915
War Diary	Busseboom	06/08/1915	10/08/1915
War Diary	Trenches	11/08/1915	18/08/1915
War Diary	Busseboom	19/08/1915	23/08/1915
War Diary	Spoil Bank	24/08/1915	28/08/1915
War Diary	Trenches	27/08/1915	31/08/1915
Heading	139th Inf. Bde. 46th Div. 5th Battn. The Sherwood Foresters (Nottinghamshire And Derbyshire Regiment). September 1915		
War Diary	Trenches astride the Comines Canal South of Ypres	01/09/1915	03/09/1915
War Diary	Busseboom	04/09/1915	09/09/1915
War Diary	Trenches as above	10/09/1915	16/09/1915
War Diary	Supports Canal Bank	17/09/1915	22/09/1915
War Diary	Trenches	23/09/1915	28/09/1915
War Diary	Busseboom	29/09/1915	29/09/1915
War Diary	Bethune	30/09/1915	30/09/1915
Heading	139th Inf. Bde. 46th Div. 5th Battn. The Sherwood Foresters (Nottinghamshire And Derbyshire Regiment). October 1915		
War Diary	Bethune	01/10/1915	01/10/1915
War Diary	Hinges	02/10/1915	04/10/1915
War Diary	Vermelles	05/10/1915	05/10/1915
War Diary	Mazingarbe	06/10/1915	06/10/1915
War Diary	Fouquieres	07/10/1915	11/10/1915
War Diary	Vermelles	12/10/1915	15/10/1915
War Diary	Verquin	16/10/1915	18/10/1915
War Diary	Lapugnoy	19/10/1915	25/10/1915
War Diary	Bethune	26/10/1918	31/10/1918
Heading	139th Inf. Bde. 46th Div. 5th Battn. The Sherwood Foresters (Nottinghamshire And Derbyshire Regiment). November 1915		
War Diary	Bethune	01/11/1915	03/11/1915
War Diary	Paradis	04/11/1915	04/11/1915
War Diary	Lacouture	05/11/1915	05/11/1915
War Diary	Trenches	06/11/1915	09/11/1915
War Diary	Billets	10/11/1915	13/11/1915
War Diary	Trenches	14/11/1915	18/11/1915
War Diary	Billets Vielle Chapelle	19/11/1915	22/11/1915
War Diary	Trenches	23/11/1915	27/11/1915
War Diary	Richebourg St Vaast	28/11/1915	30/11/1915

Heading	139th Inf. Bde. 46th Div. 5th Battn. The Sherwood Foresters (Nottinghamshire And Derbyshire Regiment). December 1915		
War Diary	Lacouture and Richebourg St Vaast	01/12/1915	03/12/1915
War Diary	La Motte Baudet	04/12/1915	18/12/1915
War Diary	Near Widdebrouck	19/12/1915	25/12/1915
War Diary	Molinghem	26/12/1915	31/12/1915
Heading	1/5th Notts & Derby Jan 1916 Vol IX 46		
War Diary	Molinghem	01/01/1916	08/01/1916
War Diary	Marseilles	09/01/1916	26/01/1916
War Diary	Gorenflos	27/01/1916	31/01/1916
War Diary	Gorenflos	01/02/1916	09/02/1916
War Diary	Bernaville	10/02/1916	16/02/1916
War Diary	Mailly Maillet	16/02/1916	28/02/1916
War Diary	Louvencourt	29/02/1916	01/03/1916
War Diary	Gezaincourt	02/03/1916	06/03/1916
War Diary	Berlencourt	07/03/1916	31/03/1916
War Diary	Acq.	01/04/1916	30/04/1916
War Diary	Auxi-Le-Chateau	01/05/1916	31/05/1916
Miscellaneous	1/5 N & D June 1916	18/06/1916	18/06/1916
War Diary	Fonquevillers	01/06/1916	30/06/1916
Miscellaneous			
Miscellaneous	1st July 1916 (46th Division).	01/07/1916	01/07/1916
War Diary	Fonquevillers	01/07/1916	30/07/1916
Miscellaneous	To Headquarters, 139th Infantry Brigade.	03/09/1916	03/09/1916
War Diary	Bellacourt	01/08/1916	30/09/1916
War Diary	Trenches Grosville	01/10/1916	31/10/1916
War Diary	Sus. St. Leger	01/11/1916	30/11/1916
Miscellaneous	To Headquarters, 139th Infantry Brigade	03/01/1917	03/01/1917
War Diary	Sus. St. Leger	01/12/1916	31/12/1916
War Diary	Souastre	01/01/1917	31/01/1917
Miscellaneous	To Headquarters, 139th Infantry Brigade.	03/03/1917	03/03/1917
War Diary	Souastre	01/02/1917	28/02/1917
War Diary		01/03/1917	31/03/1917
Miscellaneous	To Headquarters, 139th Infantry Brigade.	04/05/1917	04/05/1917
War Diary	Rely	01/04/1917	30/04/1917
Miscellaneous	To Headquarters, 139th Infantry Brigade	03/06/1917	03/06/1917
War Diary	Bully Grenay	01/05/1917	31/05/1917
War Diary	Lievin	01/06/1917	30/06/1917
War Diary	Cite St. Theodore	01/07/1917	31/07/1917
War Diary	Cite St Elie	01/08/1917	31/08/1917
War Diary	Annequin	01/09/1917	30/09/1917
War Diary	Hill to Sector Loos	01/10/1917	14/11/1917
War Diary	Novelles	14/11/1917	15/11/1917
War Diary	N. Elie Right Sector	15/11/1917	22/11/1917
War Diary	Fooquieres	22/11/1917	27/11/1917
War Diary	Verquin	27/11/1917	28/11/1917
War Diary	St. Elie Right. Sector	28/11/1917	03/12/1917
War Diary	Verquin	03/12/1917	09/12/1917
War Diary	St Elie Right Sector	09/12/1917	15/12/1917
War Diary		11/12/1917	11/12/1917
War Diary	Philosophe	15/12/1917	21/12/1917
War Diary		18/12/1917	18/12/1917
War Diary	St Elie Right Sector	21/12/1917	27/12/1917
War Diary	Verquin	27/12/1917	03/01/1918
War Diary	St Elie Right Sector	03/01/1918	09/01/1918

War Diary	Philosophe	09/01/1918	17/01/1918
War Diary	St Elie Right Sector	17/01/1918	22/01/1918
War Diary	Lapugnoy	23/01/1918	07/02/1918
War Diary	Auchy-Au-Bois	08/02/1918	08/02/1918
War Diary	Erny St Julien	09/02/1918	04/03/1918
War Diary	Auchy-Au-Bois	05/03/1918	05/03/1918
War Diary	La Preol	06/03/1918	13/03/1918
War Diary	Cambrin Sector	14/03/1918	14/03/1918
War Diary	Beuvry	20/03/1918	23/03/1918
War Diary	Annequin	24/03/1918	25/03/1918
War Diary	Cite.St. Pierre	27/03/1918	27/03/1918
War Diary	St. Emile Sector Left Sector	28/03/1918	31/03/1918
Miscellaneous	Time Table		
Miscellaneous	1/5th Battalion, The Sherwood Foresters.	29/03/1918	29/03/1918
Heading	139th Brigade. 46th Division. 1/5th Sherwood Foresters April 1918		
War Diary	St Emile Section Left sub-Sector	01/04/1918	02/04/1918
War Diary	Cite St Pierre	03/04/1918	05/04/1918
War Diary	St Emile Section Right Sub-Sector	06/04/1918	11/04/1918
War Diary	Bully Grenay	11/04/1918	12/04/1918
War Diary	Verquin & Houchin	13/04/1918	15/04/1918
War Diary	Houchin	16/04/1918	18/04/1918
War Diary	Cambrin	19/04/1918	23/04/1918
War Diary	Beuvry	23/04/1918	23/04/1918
War Diary	Essars Section	24/04/1918	28/04/1918
War Diary	Vaudricourt	28/04/1918	02/05/1918
War Diary	Gorre Section	03/05/1918	10/05/1918
War Diary	Verquin	12/05/1918	14/05/1918
War Diary	Essars Section	14/05/1918	25/05/1918
War Diary	Vaudricourt	26/05/1918	30/05/1918
War Diary	Gorre Section	30/05/1918	07/06/1918
War Diary	Vaudricourt Wood	08/06/1918	11/06/1918
War Diary	Essars Section	11/06/1918	20/06/1918
War Diary	Verquin Vaudricourt Wood	20/06/1918	23/06/1918
War Diary	Gorre Section	23/06/1918	30/06/1918
Operation(al) Order(s)	Operation Order No. 45.	17/06/1918	17/06/1918
War Diary	Report on Raid by the 1/5th Battalion, Sherwood Foresters, on the night of 18th/19th June, 1918.	18/06/1918	18/06/1918
War Diary	Gorre Section	01/07/1918	01/07/1918
War Diary	Vaudricourt Wood	02/07/1918	05/07/1918
War Diary	Essars Section	05/07/1918	15/07/1918
War Diary	Vaudricourt Wood	16/07/1918	31/07/1918
War Diary	Essars Section	21/07/1918	02/08/1918
War Diary	Verquin Vaudricourt Wood	03/07/1918	08/07/1918
War Diary	Gorre Sector	08/08/1918	14/08/1918
War Diary	Essars Sector	15/08/1918	20/08/1918
War Diary	Vaudricourt Wood	21/08/1918	26/08/1918
War Diary	Gorre Section	26/08/1918	30/08/1918
Heading	1/5 Sherwood Forester Vol 42 Sept 1918		
Heading	War Diary D.A.G 3rd Echelon Base.		
War Diary	Gorre Sector	01/09/1918	06/09/1918
War Diary	Lapugnoy	07/09/1918	12/09/1918
War Diary	Lahoussoye	13/09/1918	19/09/1918
War Diary	Pontruet	20/09/1918	30/09/1918
Map	Note Change of Colour. Enemy Trenches in Blue		
War Diary	Lahoucourt	01/10/1918	10/10/1918

Type	Description	Start	End
War Diary	Mericourt Area	11/10/1918	13/10/1918
War Diary	Bohain	14/10/1918	18/10/1918
War Diary	Fresnoy Le Grand	19/10/1918	29/10/1918
War Diary	Bohain	30/10/1918	31/10/1918
Operation(al) Order(s)	Operation Order No 78	03/10/1918	03/10/1918
Operation(al) Order(s)	1/5th Bn. Sherwood Foresters Operation Order No. 79	05/10/1918	05/10/1918
Operation(al) Order(s)	139 Infantry Brigade Order 211	05/10/1918	05/10/1918
Miscellaneous	Officer Commanding. 5th. 6th 8th Sherwood Foresters	05/10/1918	05/10/1918
Operation(al) Order(s)	1/5 Sherwood Foresters Operation Order No. 80	07/10/1918	07/10/1918
Operation(al) Order(s)	1/5 Sherwood Foresters Operation Order No. 81	08/10/1918	08/10/1918
Operation(al) Order(s)	139th Infantry Brigade Order 203	08/10/1918	08/10/1918
Operation(al) Order(s)	Operation Order 82.	10/10/1918	10/10/1918
Operation(al) Order(s)	139 Inf. Bde Order No. 214	10/10/1918	10/10/1918
Operation(al) Order(s)	1/5th. Bn. Sherwood Foresters. Operation Order No. 83	12/10/1918	12/10/1918
Miscellaneous	Reference Operation Order No. 84.	17/10/1918	17/10/1918
Miscellaneous	Reference Operation Order No. 84.	16/10/1918	16/10/1918
Operation(al) Order(s)	Operation Order No. 84.	16/10/1918	16/10/1918
Operation(al) Order(s)	Operation Orders No. 84 A	30/10/1918	30/10/1918
War Diary	Bohain	01/11/1918	14/11/1918
War Diary	Landrecies	15/11/1918	29/11/1918
Miscellaneous	Photograph Extracted from the diary	19/11/1925	19/11/1925
Miscellaneous	A Form. Messages And Signals.		
War Diary	Landrecies	01/12/1918	11/01/1919
War Diary	Beaurepaire	11/01/1919	18/02/1919
War Diary	Catillon	19/02/1919	19/02/1919
War Diary	Bethencourt	20/02/1919	31/05/1919

war 26915(1)

war 26915(2)

46TH DIVISION
139TH INFY BDE

5TH BN NOTTS & DERBY

MAR 1915 – MAY 1919

139th Inf.Bde.
46th Div.

5th BATTN. THE SHERWOOD FORESTERS (NOTTINGHAMSHIRE
AND DERBYSHIRE REGIMENT).

M A R C H

1 9 1 5

1/5 K. Sherwood Foresters

WAR DIARY or INTELLIGENCE SUMMARY.

Army Form C. 2118.

(Erase heading not required.)

Hour, Date, Place	Summary of Events and Information	Remarks and references to Appendices
TERDEGHEM 1915		
1st March	Resting in billets	
2nd "	Transport left at 5 p.m.	Gal.
3 "	Marched to SAN SYLVESTRE (2 miles) Inspected by General Sir Horace Smith Dorrien; conveyed in motor buses to BAILLEUL (8 miles) thence marched to ROMARIN via RABOT (5 miles)	Gal.
4 "		Gal.
ROMARIN		
5 "	C Company + 1 platoon B Company in trenches for instruction with the R Warwickshire Regt and the Seaforth Highlanders; remainder trench digging and forming Grenadier Company. One casualty – Sergt J. Ware killed.	Gal.
6 "	D Company + 1 platoon B Company in trenches for instruction with the same Regiments – other parties as before	Gal.
7 "	C Company + 1 platoon B Company in trenches on left – other details again repeated. Weather improving but colder. Grenadiers digging on slope.	Gal.
8 "	Co ready to move consequently no trench party	Gal.
9 "	Marched to MERRIS via BAILLEUL (10½ miles) Billeted outside village. Orders received to be ready to move again at an hour's notice. Received information	Gal.

around 5th Br Northumb RV

1/5 Sherwood Foresters

Army Form C. 2118.

WAR DIARY
or
INTELLIGENCE SUMMARY.
(Erase heading not required.)

Instructions regarding War Diaries and Intelligence Summaries are contained in F.S. Regs., Part II. and the Staff Manual respectively. Title pages will be prepared in manuscript.

Hour, Date, Place		Summary of Events and Information	Remarks and references to Appendices
MERRIS. 1915.	10 March	That Major Marsden the remainder of the Battalion detrained at HAZEBROUCK on March 7th.	G.M.
"	11 "	Major Marsden's party located at TERDEGHEM. Orders to join the Battalion at MERRIS tomorrow. Urgent orders not to leave billets in anticipation of sudden move.	G.M.
"	"	10.50 a.m. received orders to be ready to move at 11 a.m. At 11.00 a.m. received orders to move at once. B.H. at 12 noon – marched via BLEUE, DOULIEU, TROU BAYARD and CROIX AU BAC to BAC ST MAUR (13 miles) Billetted in flax spinning mill (Major Marsden's party) around MERRIS at 11.45 a.m. rested and continued to BAC ST MAUR joining the Batt." at 10 p.m. (22 miles in all). For previous movements of Major Marsden's party see below.	G.M.
BAC ST MAUR	12 "	Stood by all day waiting orders to move.	G.M.
"	13 "	Sherwood Foresters Brigade detached from North Midland Division to join the 2nd Cavalry Division under General Gough. Left BAC ST MAUR and marched via ESTAIRES to NEUF BERQUIN.	G.M. Battle of NEUVE CHAPELLE.
NEUF BERQUIN from 14th to 31st March		Resting and training at NEUF BERQUIN. The 1st Battalion the	G.M.

Forms/C. 2118/10.

1/5th Sherwood Foresters

Army Form C. 2118.

WAR DIARY
or
INTELLIGENCE SUMMARY.
(Erase heading not required.)

Instructions regarding War Diaries and Intelligence Summaries are contained in F.S. Regs., Part II. and the Staff Manual respectively. Title pages will be prepared in manuscript.

Hour, Date, Place		Summary of Events and Information	Remarks and references to Appendices
HAYRE			
1915.	4 March	Major Heaton at Rest Camp. Capt Clay at N°6 Stan.	Col.
"	5 "	Both parties returned to HAYRE.	Col.
"	6 "	Detrained at HAZEBROUCK and marched to TERDEGHEM	Col.
TERDEGHEM			
"	7 "	Billeted at TERDEGHEM.	Col.
"	8 "	At TERDEGHEM.	Col.
"	9 "	} Marched to join the rest of the Battalion at MERRIS according to orders received.	Col.
"	10 "		
"	11 "		Col.
		End of note re Movements of detachment.	

S. Huxley Major
Comm'd 1/5 D: Notts & Derby Regt

139th Inf.Bde.
46th Div.

5th BATTN. THE SHERWOOD FORESTERS (NOTTINGHAMSHIRE AND DERBYSHIRE REGIMENT).

A P R I L

1 9 1 5

5th Sherwood Foresters

Army Form C. 2118.

WAR DIARY
INTELLIGENCE SUMMARY.
(Erase heading not required.)

Instructions regarding War Diaries and Intelligence Summaries are contained in F. S. Regs., Part II. and the Staff Manual respectively. Title pages will be prepared in manuscript.

Hour, Date, Place		Summary of Events and Information	Remarks and references to Appendices
NEUF BERQUIN			
1915. April	1st	Resting.	GAR.
"	2nd	Left NEUF BERQUIN and marched about 5½ miles, billetting for the night in various farms about 1½ miles S.W. of BAILLEUL.	GOOD FRIDAY. GAR.
"	3rd	Marched to BAILLEUL — Billetted in the RUE DE LA GARE.	L'Hutfeld. GAR.
BAILLEUL "	4th	Church Parade for 400 men in the Musée.	EASTER SUNDAY. GAR.
"	5th	Marched to LOCRE — 4 miles — to take over sector of trenches. Billetted in village — school for 1½ Companies; remainder in wooden huts on BAILLEUL road.	GAR.
LOCRE	6th		
"	7th	Resting at LOCRE. GAR.	
"	8th		
"	9th	Lt. Col. G. Mosley left on sick leave. Battalion marched at night to take charge of F sector of trenches under command of Major G.A. Kirwan. Headquarters at LINDENHOECK, relieving the 7th Sherwood Foresters. Two Companies forming firing line & supports, and two Companies in reserve. GAR.	
LINDENHOECK	10th		
"	11th	In F sector of trenches. GAR.	
"	12th		

E.S. Cox Major

5th Sherwood Foresters

Army Form C. 2118.

WAR DIARY
or
INTELLIGENCE SUMMARY.
(Erase heading not required.)

Instructions regarding War Diaries and Intelligence Summaries are contained in F. S. Regs., Part II. and the Staff Manual respectively. Title pages will be prepared in manuscript.

Hour, Date, Place	Summary of Events and Information	Remarks and references to Appendices
LINDENHOECK 1915. April 13th	7th Battalion relieved the 5th Battalion - latter returned to rest at LOCRE. Casualties during period - 3 killed, and 9 wounded, of whom 1 subsequently died of wounds. GAL	
LOCRE " 14th " 15th " 16th " 17th	Resting at LOCRE. Major E.S.D'E. Coke C.M.G. of the King's own Scottish Borderers took command on the 14th. GAL	
LINDENHOECK " 18th " 19th " 20th " 21st " 22nd " 23rd	Returned to trenches GAL. In trenches. Casualties during period 2 killed and 10 wounded, including Capt/Adjutant W. Mosley, and 2 Lieut Stebbing. GAL. Left trenches and bivouacked at LINDENHOECK. GAL.	
LOCRE " 24th " 25th " 26th " 27th	Returned to LOCRE GAL. Resting at LOCRE GAL. Returned to trenches at LINDENHOECK. GAL.	

E.S.Coke, Major.

5th Sherwood Foresters

Army Form C. 2118.

WAR DIARY
INTELLIGENCE SUMMARY.
(Erase heading not required.)

Instructions regarding War Diaries and Intelligence Summaries are contained in F. S. Regs., Part II. and the Staff Manual respectively. Title pages will be prepared in manuscript.

Hour, Date, Place	Summary of Events and Information	Remarks and references to Appendices
LINDENHOECK. 1915. April 28th	Took over G1, G2 and G6 trenches in addition to the trenches already held by us, necessitating 3 Companies in future being in the trenches and one in support. A German countermine penetrated into our mine in front of G.2 and was blown up. We fired 6" Trench Mortar from behind F.6. Damage unknown. G.O.C.	
" " 29th 30th	In trenches. Casualties during period 2 killed & 12 wounded of whom 1 subsequently died of wounds. G.O.C.	

E.S. Cox Major.

139th Inf.Bde.
46th Div.

5th BATTN. THE SHERWOOD FORESTERS (NOTTINGHAMSHIRE
AND DERBYSHIRE REGIMENT).

M A Y

1 9 1 5

5th Sherwood Foresters

Army Form C. 2118.

WAR DIARY
or
INTELLIGENCE SUMMARY.
(Erase heading not required.)

Hour, Date, Place			Summary of Events and Information	Remarks and References to Appendices
LOCRE	1915			
Saturday	May 1st		Back to LOCRE from trenches	GAL
Sunday	"	2nd	Resting at LOCRE	GAL
Monday	"	3rd		
Tuesday	"	4th	Back to trenches at LINDENHOECK	GAL
Wednesday	"	5th		
LINDENHOECK				
Thursday	"	6th	In trenches at "LINDENHOEK"	GAL
Friday	"	7th		
Saturday	"	8th	We exploded a mine under the German trenches opposite G2 - action not followed up.	GAL
Sunday	"	9th		
Monday	"	10th	Another mine exploded in front of G2 by Enemy who damaged their own wire trenches - not followed up. Returned to rest at LOCRE, the 5th Lincolns taking over trenches. Casualties 4 killed, 26 wounded.	GAL
LOCRE				
Tuesday	"	11th	Went to farms & bivouacs near KEMMEL.	GAL
Wednesday	"	12th	Resting	GAL
Thursday	"	13th	Took over following trenches from the 6th Sherwood Foresters - J3R, J3L, J3A, J4, J11, S6, K1, K1A, K1B, K2, K2A, K2B, K3, L1, L2, L3, L4 & L6. Headquarters at ROSSIGNOL.	GAL GAL GAL GAL

5th Sherwood Foresters

Army Form C. 2118.

WAR DIARY
or
INTELLIGENCE SUMMARY.
(Erase heading not required.)

Instructions regarding War Diaries and Intelligence Summaries are contained in F. S. Regs., Part II. and the Staff Manual respectively. Title pages will be prepared in manuscript.

Hour, Date, Place	Summary of Events and Information	Remarks and References to Appendices
ROSSIGNOL 1915		
Friday May 14th }	In trenches — 3 Companies in trenches & one in support. GAH	
Saturday " 15th }		
Sunday " 16th }		
LITTLE KEMMEL		
Monday " 17th }	Moved back to billets & bivouacs. Same as before. Casualties 5 killed and 19 wounded including Captain H.J. Colas. GAH	
Tuesday " 18th }	Resting. GAH	
Wednesday " 19th }		
Thursday " 20th }		
ROSSIGNOL		
Friday " 21st	Back to trenches. Firing up J3R, J3A and Deb. post to the troops on our right. Major E.S. Coke left to take command of the 2nd K.O.S.B. Major Lewis placed in command. GAH	
Saturday " 22nd }	In trenches. GAH	
Sunday " 23rd }		
Monday " 24th }		

G A Lewis
Lt Col

3rd Sherwood Foresters

Army Form C. 2118.

WAR DIARY
or
INTELLIGENCE SUMMARY.
(Erase heading not required.)

Hour, Date, Place	Summary of Events and Information	Remarks and References to Appendices
LITTLE KEMMEL 1915		
Tuesday May 25th	Back to same bivouac — Casualties none killed — 14 wounded	
Wednesday " 26th		
Thursday " 27th	Resting — making (new huts) shelters —	
Friday " 28th		
Saturday " 29th		
ROSSIGNOL Sunday " 30th	Back to same trenches as before	
Monday " 31st	In trenches —	

C. Abeer Lt Col.

139th Inf.Bde.
46th Div.

5th BATTN. THE SHERWOOD FORESTERS (NOTTINGHAMSHIRE AND DERBYSHIRE REGIMENT).

J U N E

1 9 1 5

Army Form C. 2118.

WAR DIARY
or
INTELLIGENCE SUMMARY.
(*Erase heading not required.*)

Hour, Date, Place	Summary of Events and Information	Remarks and References to Appendices
	Confidential
War Diary
of
1/5th Bn. Sherwood Foresters
From 1st June 1915 to 30th June 1915.	

Instructions regarding War Diaries and Intelligence Summaries are contained in F. S. Regs., Part II. and the Staff Manual respectively. Title pages will be prepared in manuscript.

Army Form C. 2118.

5th Sherwood Foresters

WAR DIARY
or
INTELLIGENCE SUMMARY.
(Erase heading not required.)

Instructions regarding War Diaries and Intelligence Summaries are contained in F. S. Regs., Part II. and the Staff Manual respectively. Title pages will be prepared in manuscript.

Hour, Date, Place	Summary of Events and Information	Remarks and References to Appendices
NORTH OF KEMMEL		
Tuesday 1st June	In trenches. GAL.	
Wednesday 2nd "	Gave up following trenches to 7th & 8th Battalions S.F.; J3L, J4, J5, J6. Took on L5, L7A, L7B, L7C, M1 and M5 from 3rd Worcesters. K1 and K1A. Retaining about the intervening trenches. A Company of 8th K.R.R. attached for instruction. GAL.	
LITTLE KEMMEL		
Thursday 3rd "	Relieved to bivouac at LITTLE KEMMEL. Casualties during tour GAL. KILLED 4, WOUNDED 9, including Major Worsley, Lieuts Elliott & Pryor.	
Friday 4th "	} Resting in same bivouac GAL	
Saturday 5th "		
Sunday 6th "		
Monday 7th "		
TRENCHES		
Tuesday 8th "	} Back to same trenches GAL	
Wednesday 9th "		
Thursday 10th "	} In trenches - a Company of the Shropshire Light Infantry attached for instruction. GAL.	
Friday 11th "		
LITTLE KEMMEL		
Saturday 12th "	Back to same bivouac - Casualties KILLED 2, WOUNDED 1. GAL.	
Sunday 13th "	} In bivouac. GAL.	GAK(?) Lt Col
Monday 14th "		
Tuesday 15th "		

5th Sherwood Foresters

Army Form C. 2118.

WAR DIARY
or
INTELLIGENCE SUMMARY.
(Erase heading not required.)

Hour, Date, Place	Summary of Events and Information	Remarks and References to Appendices
TRENCHES		
Wednesday June 16th	Back to same trenches. A Company of the King's Own Yorkshire Light Infantry attached for instruction. GAL	
Thursday " 17th		
Friday " 18th	In trenches – Casualties during tour KILLED 1, WOUNDED 12. GAL	
Saturday " 19th	Relieved by the 1st York & Lancaster Regt: marched to LOCRE and bivouacked in field WEST of Church. GAL	
LOCRE Sunday " 20th		
	5 – 17th Battalion S.F. addressed & complimented by General Sir Charles Ferguson. Marched at night via OUDERDOM to a group of huts about one mile S.W. of VLAMERTINGHE. Distance about 7 miles. GAL	
VLAMERTINGHE		
Monday " 21st	Resting GAL	
Tuesday " 22nd		
ZILLEBEKE		
Wednesday " 23rd	Marched via KRUISSTRAAT to trenches East of ZILLEBEKE. Bivouacked in SANCTUARY WOOD, acting as supports to the 6th & 8th Sh. For. GAL	
Thursday " 24th	In SANCTUARY WOOD – rebuilding outpost trenches old ones Bursting shell on the 26th killed Regt: HAYES & six others, & wounded 12 more. GAL	
Friday " 25th		
Saturday " 26th		
Sunday " 27th		
Monday " 28th		

GALewon Lt Col

5th Sherwood Foresters

Army Form C. 2118.

WAR DIARY
or
INTELLIGENCE SUMMARY.
(Erase heading not required.)

Instructions regarding War Diaries and Intelligence Summaries are contained in F. S. Regs., Part II. and the Staff Manual respectively. Title pages will be prepared in manuscript.

Hour, Date, Place	Summary of Events and Information	Remarks and References to Appendices
POPERINGHE Tuesday 29th June	Left SANCTUARY WOOD and marched to a farm at G.26 A.1.9. about 2 miles SOUTH of POPERINGHE. Bivouacked in field. Marched about 15 miles. Casualties KILLED 9, WOUNDED 16, including Lt S Mallen. G.A.	G.A. Wingfield
Wednesday 30th "	Resting - Training, building bivouacs, fitting mill to - G.A.	G.A. Wingfield

139th Inf.Bde.
46th Div.

5th BATTN. THE SHERWOOD FORESTERS (NOTTINGHAMSHIRE AND DERBYSHIRE REGIMENT).

J U L Y

1 9 1 5

Army Form C. 2118.

WAR DIARY
or
INTELLIGENCE SUMMARY.

(Erase heading not required.)

Instructions regarding War Diaries and Intelligence Summaries are contained in F. S. Regs., Part II. and the Staff Manual respectively. Title pages will be prepared in manuscript.

Hour, Date, Place	Summary of Events and Information	Remarks and references to Appendices

Confidential

War Diary

of

15th. Bn: The Sherwood Foresters.

from 1st July 1915. to 31st July 1915.

5th Sherwood Foresters
Army Form C. 2118.

WAR DIARY or INTELLIGENCE SUMMARY.
(Erase heading not required.)

Hour, Date, Place	Summary of Events and Information	Remarks and references to Appendices
NEAR BUSSEBOOM. G.26.a.1.9. Thursday July 1st 1915 Saturday " 10th " Sunday " 11th "	Bivouacking - resting & training. G.A.L.	
TRENCHES around SANCTUARY WOOD To Sunday " 18th "	Marched via BUSSEBOOM and KRUISSTRAAT to trenches East of ZILLEBEKE, taking over trenches A9, S0, A1, A2, A3, A4, A5 from 5th Leicesters. Half for 2 hours on way - distance 15 miles - All men in trenches, including some in support trenches close up. G.A.L. In trenches - 3 wet days - running suspected in A9 & S0 - casualties by sniping. Casualties during two 2 killed - 12 wounded, including Lieuts RUDGARD, GILCHRIST and ROBOTHAM. G.A.L. Moved another bay to trenches slightly to North, taking over trenches from 6/S Batt⁵ & partly from ⁷ Batt⁵ Sherwood Foresters, trenches A8, A9, A10, A11, A12, B1 & B2. All men in trenches. HQrs close by in SANCTUARY WOOD. G.A.L. Casualties to this date 2 killed - 12 wounded, the latter including Lieuts RUDGARD, GILCHRIST and ROBOTHAM. G.A.L.	
TRENCHES To Saturday July 24th " Sunday " 25th "	In above trenches - no particular items of interest - reliefs from trenches on this day to dug-outs in MAPLE COPSE in close support, changing places with the 6th Sherwood Foresters, who returned in. G.A.L. An enemy aeroplane was brought down in flames within 100 yards. G.A.L.	G.A.L. E. W. G.A.L.

(9 29 6) W 3332-1107 100,000 10/13 H W V Forms/C. 2118/10.

5th Sherwood Foresters

Army Form C. 2118.

WAR DIARY
or
INTELLIGENCE SUMMARY.
(Erase heading not required.)

Instructions regarding War Diaries and Intelligence Summaries are contained in F.S. Regs., Part II. and the Staff Manual respectively. Title pages will be prepared in manuscript.

Hour, Date, Place	Summary of Events and Information	Remarks and references to Appendices
MAPLE COPSE To Friday July 30th 1915.	of MAPLE COPSE — our ?ranger jumped out from a great height into SANCTUARY WOOD and the pilot was found burnt to death in seat where the flames had subsided. GAK. Remained in MAPLE COPSE. No further items of interest. In the day the Battⁿ returned to same trenches as before, relieving the 6th Sherwood Foresters - GAK.	
TRENCHES Saturday " 31st "	Enemy attacked HOOGE on our left flank at 2.15 a.m. with liquid fire and by daylight had secured the ridge overlooking our H.Q^{rs}, and SANCTUARY WOOD. Their fire could be turned into the rear of the Battⁿ, & the trenches are only hidden by the trees. Places on 2 support machine guns in position near H.Q^{rs} where they was action a considerable time. Our Battⁿ was not affected, but the new line was formed by the K.R.R's & R.B.'s on the East side of ZOUAVE WOOD and SANCTUARY WOOD. GAK. At 2.45 p.m. the same brigade made a counter attack after ½ an hour artillery preparation. This not with no success. Gun machine GAK.	

E.A. Kerr Lt Col.

5th Sherwood Foresters

Army Form C. 2118.

WAR DIARY
or
INTELLIGENCE SUMMARY.

(Erase heading not required.)

Instructions regarding War Diaries and Intelligence Summaries are contained in F.S. Regs., Part II. and the Staff Manual respectively. Title pages will be prepared in manuscript.

Hour, Date, Place	Summary of Events and Information	Remarks and references to Appendices
	Guns again co-operated. AAA. At 9.0 p.m. a further attack was made by the enemy on a considerable front, but it was all repulsed by 11 p.m. AAA. Further casualties to end of month KILLED 12 WOUNDED 34 AAA	

139th Inf.Bde.
46th Div.

5th BATTN. THE SHERWOOD FORESTERS (NOTTINGHAMSHIRE AND DERBYSHIRE REGIMENT).

A U G U S T

1 9 1 5

Army Form C. 2118.

5th Shenwood Foresters

WAR DIARY
or
INTELLIGENCE SUMMARY.
(Erase heading not required.)

Instructions regarding War Diaries and Intelligence Summaries are contained in F.S. Regs., Part II. and the Staff Manual respectively. Title pages will be prepared in manuscript.

Hour, Date, Place	Summary of Events and Information	Remarks and references to Appendices
IN TRENCHES AROUND SANCTUARY WOOD about 1 mile S. of HOOGE SUNDAY 1st August 1915 to THURSDAY 5"	Constant artillery fire by our artillery on HOOGE — daily/continuous by 6th Division preparatory to proposed attack on HOOGE. Enemy quiet on our immediate front. GAK	
BUSSEBOOM FRIDAY 6th August 1915 SATURDAY 7 " " SUNDAY 8 " " MONDAY 9 " " TUESDAY 10 " "	Relieved on THURSDAY 5/8/15 by 6th Sherwood Foresters & 2nd Sherwood Foresters relieved us from MAPLE COPSE — 2nd Sherwood Foresters relieved at MAPLE COPSE, when we marched to post billets at BUSSEBOOM. Casualties during tour KILLED O, WOUNDED 9. GAK Resting. GAK	
TRENCHES WEDNESDAY 11 " "	Relieved 7 Sherwood Foresters in SANCTUARY WOOD — taking on B3 trench & finding 60 men & half in B4 trench. One Company for trenches also in R2 Switch trench Moreover R1 & R3, strong posts in reserve. GAK	STRENGTH. Off. 24 men 811
THURSDAY 12 " "	Took on half of B4 trench. GAK	21 625

G. Aiken Lt. Col.

Army Form C. 2118.

5th Sherwood Foresters

WAR DIARY
OR
INTELLIGENCE SUMMARY.
(Erase heading not required.)

Hour, Date, Place	Summary of Events and Information	Remarks and references to Appendices
Friday 13 August 1915 to Wednesday 18	In trenches — uneventful period. Casualties during tour Killed 2, Wounded 14. G.A.K.	
BUSSEBOOM Thursday 19	Relieved by 1st Royal Scots Fusiliers — returned to pr of billets at Busseboom. G.A.K.	
Friday 20	" "	
Saturday 21	" "	
Sunday 22	" "	
Monday 23	In Rest Camp G.A.K.	
SPOILBANK Tuesday 24	Proceeded via KRUISSTRAAT to take over new trenches on left South side of the COMINES CANAL SE of YPRES. In support for the first period of 6 days, one Company south of Canal + 3 north of Canal — all in dugouts. Took over from the 1st GORDON HIGHLANDERS. G.A.K.	25/8/15 Off. Men STRENGTH 24 807 For Trench 19 573
Wednesday 25	In support, working on Communication trenches &c.	
Thursday 26	"	
Friday 27	Casualties Killed 1 Wounded 5 G.A.K.	
Saturday 28	"	
Trenches 27, 28, & 29 Sunday 29	Relieved 6th Sherwood Foresters in trenches 27, 28, & 29, also	G. A. [illegible] Lt Col

Army Form C. 2118.

5th Sherwood Foresters

WAR DIARY
or
INTELLIGENCE SUMMARY.
(Erase heading not required.)

Hour, Date, Place	Summary of Events and Information	Remarks and references to Appendices
MONDAY 30 August 1915	Various support trenches. Headquarters on SOUTH BANK of CONINES CANAL. Improvement of work general. Trenches - communication trenches in hill LSP for comfort. Rifle fire - wastcher from an in trench tottery trig construction - Corps of Engineers formed by Brigade. AK.	
TUESDAY 31 " "	In trenches. GA	GA Lewis Lt Col
	Sick Evacuated during the month 21. GA	

139th Inf.Bde.
46th Div.

5th BATTN. THE SHERWOOD FORESTERS (NOTTINGHAMSHIRE
AND DERBYSHIRE REGIMENT).

S E P T E M B E R

1 9 1 5

Army Form C. 2118.

5th Sherwood Foresters

WAR DIARY
or
INTELLIGENCE SUMMARY.
(Erase heading not required.)

Hour, Date, Place	Summary of Events and Information	Remarks and references to Appendices
TRENCHES astride the COMINES CANAL South of YPRES		
WEDNESDAY 1st Sept 1915	In trenches GAL	Strength on 1/9/15 O.R. 793. GAL Off. 24
THURSDAY 2 " "	In trenches – weather bad – GAL	
FRIDAY 3 " "		
BUSSEBOOM		
SATURDAY 4 " "	Relieved by 6th Sherwood Foresters & returned to our Rest Camp near BUSSEBOOM. Weather improving. Casualties during tour: KILLED 0 WOUNDED 2. GAL	
SUNDAY 5 " "		
MONDAY 6 " "	In Rest Camp – fine fine French GAL	
TUESDAY 7 " "		
WEDNESDAY 8 " "		
THURSDAY 9 " "		
TRENCHES as above		
FRIDAY 10 " "	Back to same trenches astride the canal GAL	Strength 10/9/15 O.R. 766 Off. 24 G A Lewis
SATURDAY 11 " "		
SUNDAY 12 " "	In trenches GAL	
MONDAY 13 " "		

Army Form C. 2118.

5th Sherwood Foresters

WAR DIARY
or
INTELLIGENCE SUMMARY.

(Erase heading not required.)

Instructions regarding War Diaries and Intelligence Summaries are contained in F. S. Regs., Part II. and the Staff Manual respectively. Title pages will be prepared in manuscript.

Hour, Date, Place	Summary of Events and Information	Remarks and references to Appendices
TUESDAY 14 Sept 1915	In trenches. GAK	
WEDNESDAY 15 " "	Relieved by 6th Sherwood Foresters & returned to dug-out	
THURSDAY 16 " "	and huts to act as support battalion. GAK	
SUPPORT BATTALION		
FRIDAY 17 " "	} In support. GAK	
SATURDAY 18 " "		
SUNDAY 19 " "		
MONDAY 20 " "		
TUESDAY 21 " "	Relieved the 6th Sherwood Foresters & occupied same	
WEDNESDAY 22 " "	trenches again. GAK	
TRENCHES.		
THURSDAY 23 " "	Hard at work improving splinter proof cover in view of	
FRIDAY 24 " "	attack to be made on 25/9/15. GAK	
SATURDAY 25 " "	Artillery bombardment commenced at 3 a.m. stead to till 9 a.m. Smoke attack & general first attack in early morning with a view of securing the big movement taking place further to the south. GAK	
SUNDAY 26 " "	In same trenches all quiet. GAK	

A. Henson Lt.Col.

WAR DIARY or INTELLIGENCE SUMMARY.

5th Shanwood Foresters

Army Form C. 2118.

(Erase heading not required.)

Hour, Date, Place	Summary of Events and Information	Remarks and references to Appendices
MONDAY 27 Sept 1915	In same trenches. GAL	
TUESDAY 28 " "	Left trenches & proceeded to Rest Camp near Busseboom. GAt. Casualties Killed 5 Wounded 19.	
BUSSEBOOM WEDNESDAY 29 " "	Rest Camp. GAL	Strength 29/9/15 Off 23 O.R. 746 GAL
BETHUNE THURSDAY 30 " "	Transferred from V th to XI th Corps. Inspected by Sir R. Allenby who informed us regiment leaving for new command. Marched to ABEELE station entrained 10 am & proceeded by train to FOUQUEREILLES station arriving about 10 p.m. Marched from there to BETHUNE where we billeted in the MONTMORENCY BARRACKS. GAL. Sick evacuated during month 28. GAL	

G.A.W. [signature]

139th Inf.Bde.
46th Div.

5th BATTN. THE SHERWOOD FORESTERS (NOTTINGHAMSHIRE
AND DERBYSHIRE REGIMENT).

OCTOBER

1915

Army Form C. 2118.

5th Sherwood Foresters

WAR DIARY
or
INTELLIGENCE SUMMARY.
(Erase heading not required.)

Instructions regarding War Diaries and Intelligence Summaries are contained in F. S. Regs., Part II. and the Staff Manual respectively. Title pages will be prepared in manuscript.

Place	Hour, Date	Summary of Events and Information	Remarks and References to Appendices
BETHUNE	1st Octr 1915	Billeting in Barracks. GAL	
HINGES	2nd " "	Marched from BETHUNE to HINGES, billetting in the canal area W4, W10 + W11. Billeting in various farms near at HINGES. GAL	Map reference BETHUNE contoured sheet E 30a. 36 a, SE, 36 SW 36 b, NE, 36 NW
	3rd " "	Marched in afternoon to VENDIN-LEZ-BETHUNE. Busses conveyed the	
	4th " "	Brigade to SAILLY-LABOURSE and thence marched via NOYELLES-LES-VERMELLES to occupy the German trenches captured in September, situated about G23j and east of VERMELLES. GAL	Casualties Killed 1 Wounded 3
VERMELLES	5th " "	Occupied trench and worked on turning team round. Marched at night to MAZINGARBE and billeted there the night. L23A. GAL	GOff OR 24/743
MAZINGARBE	6th " "	Marched today via NOEUX-LES-MINES to FOUQUIÈRES-LES-BETHUNE, billetting in E20b, and E21a. Reinforcement 12 arrived. GAL	Strength
FOUQUIÈRES	7th " "	} Sa billets, training + resting. GAL	
	8th " "		
	11th " "		
VERMELLES	12th " "	Marched to take part in the fight for FOSSIE No 8. Occupied LANCASHIRE TRENCH, about G2d by evening. Notts+Derby Brigade in reserve - the Battn in rear line of trenches. GAL	Total struck Trench " Off. OR 22 753 17 603
	13th " "	Ordered to move to the front about 4.15 p.m. Fight commenced at noon C.T. badly blocked, but arrived at the K trenches about G4 at midnight. One GAL	

Army Form C. 2118.

5th Sherwood Foresters

WAR DIARY
or
INTELLIGENCE SUMMARY.
(Erase heading not required.)

Instructions regarding War Diaries and Intelligence Summaries are contained in F. S. Regs., Part II. and the Staff Manual respectively. Title pages will be prepared in manuscript.

Hour, Date, Place	Summary of Events and Information	Remarks and References to Appendices
14 October 1915.	A Company under Capt KERR pent off at 1.30 a.m. to assist Bombing attack on Big Willie on right flank — B & D had previously been detached for fatigue work. C Company under Capt Chicken sent into HOHENZOLLERN Redoubt about 6 a.m., accompanied by Major Chandos & Capt Wragge. Got into touch with D Company & Capt Naylor during afternoon. Helped to hold redoubt that day. GdL.	Casualties KILLED 5 WOUNDED 42
15th " "	As the 6th S.F. could not arrive, was ordered to relieve Capt (Chicken) in the Redoubt & take Command. German Team counted bombs of 5th Battn S.F. and party of 6th S.F., with Grenadier Guards on our front. Imperial trench trampled, burnt dead & held trench all day. Enemy attacked at 9.15 p.m., but were repulsed. Relieved by 1st Coldstream Guards at 9.30 p.m. GdL.	
VERQUIN 16th " "	Battalion reassembled in field about L4 for tea at about 2.30 a.m. marched at 4.30, and arrived at VERQUIN and billetted there - E 29 c. GdL.	Receive 50 reinforcements
17th } " " 18th }	At VERQUIN resting	Receive 90 reinforcements.
LAPUGNOY 19th " " 20th " " to 25th	Moved by road to LAPUGNOY and billetted in farms &c - D 20. Received training of townsmen &c -GbL. At LAPUGNOY GbL	Casualties - Bomb accident KILLED 2 WOUNDED 4

G.C. Wien 2 Col

Army Form C. 2118.

5th Sherwood Foresters

WAR DIARY
or
INTELLIGENCE SUMMARY.
(Erase heading not required.)

Hour, Date, Place	Summary of Events and Information	Remarks and References to Appendices
BETHUNE 26th October 1915	Marched to BETHUNE and billetted about 6.11 a.m. G.d.	
27th " "	This & following days occupied in rehearsals for the inspection by H.M. THE KING. G.d.	
28th " "	Inspection of troops by H.M. THE KING OF ENGLAND the accident occurred about 10 minutes after the inspection took place in field about 1/6, say 1 mile SW of HESDIGNEUL. G.d.	Sick Evacuated during the month of October 36 G.d.
29th " "		
30th " "	In billets at BETHUNE. G.d.	
31st " "		

G A Newsree.

139th Inf.Bde.
46th Div.

5th BATTN. THE SHERWOOD FORESTERS (NOTTINGHAMSHIRE
AND DERBYSHIRE REGIMENT).

N O V E M B E R

1 9 1 5

Army Form C. 2118.

WAR DIARY
or
INTELLIGENCE SUMMARY.
(Erase heading not required.)

5th Sherwood Foresters

Hour, Date, Place	Summary of Events and Information	Remarks and References to Appendices
BETHUNE 1st Novr 1915	In billets at BETHUNE. GAL	Strength 3/11/15
2nd " "		OFF. O.R.
3rd " "		Total 22 791 GAL
PARADIS 4th " "	Moved to PARADIS preparatory to taking over new line of trenches situated in Q18c. GAL	Casualty 4/11/15
LACOUTURE 5th " "	Moved and billetted in farm between VIEILLE CHAPELLE and LACOUTURE. GAL	WOUNDED 1 O.R.
Trenches 6th " "	Took over trenches about 5.15, relieving the Headquarters in ALBERT ROAD at S8b 6.0. Two companies in front line, one in support town proper. Trenches very wet, practically unapproachable by day. GAL	Casualties KILLED 1 WOUNDED 3 O.R.
7th " "	In trenches. GAL	
8th " "		
9th " "		
Billets 10th " "	Relieved by 6th Sherwoods, and went into billets in RUE DE CAVATTES, X5 + X11. GAL	
11th " "		
12th " "	In billets as above. GAL	
13th " "		
Trenches 14th " "	Moved into trenches in S15 and S10, including the BOARS HEAD. GAL	Received reinforcements 88 O.R. GAL

Army Form C. 2118.

WAR DIARY
or
INTELLIGENCE SUMMARY.
(Erase heading not required.)

5th Sherwood Foresters

Hour, Date, Place	Summary of Events and Information	Remarks and References to Appendices
Trenches 15th Nov 1915	Two companies in front line, one in support along y Post Hound No 1. S3c50. HQrs Quarters in EDWARD ROAD — S9a76. Trenches very wet — 3'6" deep in water — Right sector only held by small posts. GAH	Casualties Killed 3 Wounded 3 GAH
16th " "	In trenches. GAH	
17th " "	" GAH	
18th " "	" GAH	
Billets 19th " "	Relieved by 8th Sherwoods & went into billets at VIEILLE CHAPELLE. GAH	
VIEILLE CHAPELLE 20th " "	" GAH	
21st " "	" GAH	
22nd " "	" GAH	
Trenches 23rd " "	Took over Trenches from the 7th Sherwoods in S10 C and S10 b. HQrs S10a 5.4. in RUE DE BOIS GAH	
24th " "	" GAH	Casualties Killed 2 GAH Wounded 2 GAH Strength 24/11/15 Off. 23 O.R. 800 GAH Total 23 800 GAH
25th " "	In trenches. GAH	
26th " "	" GAH	
27th " "	" GAH	

G A Henry Lt Col.

Army Form C. 2118.

WAR DIARY
or
INTELLIGENCE SUMMARY.

5th Sherwood Foresters

(Erase heading not required.)

Instructions regarding War Diaries and Intelligence Summaries are contained in F. S. Regs., Part II. and the Staff Manual respectively. Title pages will be prepared in manuscript.

Hour, Date, Place	Summary of Events and Information	Remarks and References to Appendices
RICHEBOURG ST VAAST 28th Nov 1915	Handed over trenches to the 8th Sherwood Foresters. Billets — 2 Companies in RICHEBOURG, and 2 Companies in X 4 c and X 4 d. G4b.	Sick evacuated during month — 84. G4b.
29th " "	In billets — G4b.	
30th " "		

G A Newno
Lt Col.

139th Inf.Bde.
46th Div.

5th BATTN. THE SHERWOOD FORESTERS (NOTTINGHAMSHIRE AND DERBYSHIRE REGIMENT).

DECEMBER

1915

December 1915

5th Sherwood Foresters

Army Form C. 2118.

WAR DIARY
or
INTELLIGENCE SUMMARY.
(Erase heading not required.)

Hour, Date, Place	Summary of Events and Information	Remarks and References to Appendices
LACOUTURE and RICHEBOURG ST VAAST. 1st Dec 1915, 2nd ", 3rd "	In rest billets - 2 Companies in each place. GCW	Strength 1/12/15 OFFICERS 22 O.R. 791 F13 / 804 GCW
LA MOTTE BAUDET 4th to 18th Decr 1915	Moved to new billets at LA MOTTE BAUDET about 2 miles N.E. of ST VENANT. GCW Company + Battalion training. GCW	
NEAR WIDDEBROUCK 19th Decr 1915 to 25th " "	Moved to new billets near WIDDEBROUCK about 2 miles N.E. of AIRE. GCW	Strength 29/12/15 OFFICERS 26 O.R. 798 / 824 GCW
MOLINGHEM 26th " " to 31st " "	Moved to new billets at MOLINGHEM about 3 miles S. of AIRE. GCW	Casualties NIL Evacuated 23 Draft joined 40 Officers " 5 Officer struck off 1. GCW

C.W. Wingfield Lt Col. C.O.

1/5th Notts + Derby

Jan 1916

Vol IX

46

Army Form C. 2118.

5th Shrews Forstrs

WAR DIARY
INTELLIGENCE SUMMARY.
(Erase heading not required.)

Instructions regarding War Diaries and Intelligence
Summaries are contained in F. S. Regs., Part II.
and the Staff Manual respectively. Title pages
will be prepared in manuscript.

Hour, Date, Place	Summary of Events and Information	Remarks and references to Appendices
1916 February January 1 to Jany 5 MOLINGHEM	In Billets at MOLINGHEM 9H7m Training under O.C. Co's. Extended order and outpost drill. 9H7m	
January 6	Entrained at BERGUETTE 9H7m	
7 & 8	Travelling	
MARSEILLES 9	Detrained MARSEILLES 9.30 a.m. marched to SANTI-CARCASSONE Camp. 9H7m	
10 to 16	Waiting orders for embarkation. Battalion trained in musketry. Bayonet fighting. Lectures to N.C.O.s 9H7m	
16 and 17	Battalion vacinated. 9H7m	
18 to 24	Waiting orders for embarkation. Scout section formed. Subalterns under 2nd in Command. Route marching Semaphore Signalling 9H7m	

G A New Lt Col

Army Form C. 2118.

WAR DIARY
INTELLIGENCE SUMMARY.
(Erase heading not required.)

5th Sherwood Foresters

Hour, Date, Place	Summary of Events and Information	Remarks and references to Appendices
1916. Jany 25. 6.30pm	2 Companies entrained at MARSEILLES 9½"	
" 26.	1 Company entrained at MARSEILLES with 6th Batt. 9½" 1 Company left behind under 2nd in Command	
" 26.	Travelling Co which was left behind entrained 9½"	
" GORENFLOS 27	Detrained at PONT REMY. 5 pm marched to GORENFLOS 9½" Billet.	January 1916. Casualties. Nil. Deaths. One. Reinforcements Officers 7 Other Ranks 96
" 28) 29)	The two other Companies arrive & join Battn. in billets 9½"	Strength of Battn. Officers 26 Other Ranks 798 For Trenches Officers 20 Other Ranks 648
" 30, 31)	Battn. inspected for venereal. 9½"	1916. Jany 5. Length of Battn Officers 33 Other Ranks 777
		1916. Feby 2. Officers 28 Other Ranks 744

G.A. Weasu
Lt Col.

Army Form C. 2118.

WAR DIARY
INTELLIGENCE SUMMARY.
(Erase heading not required.)

1/6 Sherwood Foresters February 1916.

Hour, Date, Place	Summary of Events and Information	Remarks and References to Appendices
GORENFLOS Feby 10/16 to Feby 9/16	In billets at GORENFLOS. Battalion training in Musketry, Squad & Bayonet fighting extended order drill and attack. 9H7th	February 1916. Casualties 9H7th Killed Wounded 3 7 To evacuation during Month 38 Strength - Officers - O.R. Feby 2 33 .872 (for trenches) 28 .744 Feby 25 33 820 (for trenches) 20 669 = 9H7th J.H. Hander Major Comg 1/6 Sherwood Foresters
Feby 10/16 BERNAVILLE	Marched to new billets at BERNAVILLE. 9H7th	
Feby 11th to 15.2.16	Battalion training in Musketry Grenades extended order drill and attack. 9H7th	
16th	Proceeded to MAILLY MAILLET by motor lorries and came under 36th Division. 9H7th Brigade Machine Gun Company formed. 9H7th	
MAILLY MAILLET 17th to 28th (noon)	Continuous fatigue parties of 100 men each working in 8 hour shifts carrying sandbags from Sap at K2 REDAN. 9H7th	
Noon 28th LOUVENCOURT 29th	Battalion marched to LOUVENCOURT. 9H7th In billets at LOUVENCOURT 9H7th	

Army Form C. 2118.

WAR DIARY
or
INTELLIGENCE SUMMARY.   1/5 Sherwood Foresters, March, 1916.
(Erase heading not required.)

Instructions regarding War Diaries and Intelligence Summaries are contained in F. S. Regs., Part II. and the Staff Manual respectively. Title pages will be prepared in manuscript.

1916	Hour, Date, Place		Summary of Events and Information	Remarks and References to Appendices
LOUVENCOURT	March 1st		Marched to GEZAINCOURT	S.W.
GEZAINCOURT	March 2nd		In billets	S.W.
"	3rd			
"	4th			
"	5th		Marched to BERLENCOURT. In billets	S.W.
"	6th			
"	7th		Marched to MONT ST ELOY	S.W.
"	8th			
"	9th		Relieved 152nd French Regt in the "LA FOLIE" sector	S.W.
"	10th		In trenches	S.W.
"	16th		Brigade mining section formed on 17th.	S.W.
"	17th			
"	18th		Battalion was relieved by 6th Sherwood For. & moved back to Divisional Reserve at ACQ	S.W.
"	19th		In billets	S.W.
"	20th			
"	21st			
"	22nd		Relieved 6th Sherwood Foresters in same trenches	S.W.
"	23rd		In trenches	S.W.
"	24th			
"	25th		At 12.25 am the enemy exploded a mine in front of the trenches between P74 + P75, blowing in a portion of our advanced trench at this point & immediately occupied the crater apart of the winch on each side - a protracted grenade duel took place resulting in our reoccupation of trench on each side of the crater. The crater itself was reoccupied by the enemy. An attack was made at 8pm on the crater, which gained its objective but was subsequently bombed	S.W.

WAR DIARY or INTELLIGENCE SUMMARY

Army Form C. 2118.

Hour, Date, Place	Summary of Events and Information	Remarks and References to Appendices
March 25th (cont)	bombed out of its position before it had consolidated.	
" 26th	Lt Col Lewis was relieved of the command of the Battn: Major Checkland assumed command - Lt Col Goodman & 6th Sher For" brought up 2 companies and took charge of subsequent operations. The near lip of the crater was occupied and connected up with our front line trench without opposition or casualties	Sw. Sw. Sw. Sw.
" 27th	In trenches	
" 28th	Relieved by 6th Bn Sher For 2 & moved back to ACQ	
" 29th &	Major Wilson 17th Cav I.A. assumed command of the Battalion	
" 30th & 31st	in rest billets.	Sw.

Casualties:
Killed 11*
Wounded 51
Missing 5

Men scratched during work 40

119 Reinforcements joined Batt" 19/3/16
148 " " " 30/3/16
1 Officer joined from base 31/3/16

Strength:
                Officers   O.R.
March 3rd Total   30   761 + 1 Lieut Capt Aldous
           Trench   20*   638
March 29th Total   30   949   *3 Officers at school of Instruction
           Trench   21   745

Sd/ [signature] Major
    Commdg 1/5 S[...]

Army Form C. 2118.

WAR DIARY

INTELLIGENCE SUMMARY. of 2? /7 Sherwood Foresters - April 1916.

(Erase heading not required.)

Instructions regarding War Diaries and Intelligence Summaries are contained in F. S. Regs., Part II. and the Staff Manual respectively. Title pages will be prepared in manuscript.

Hour, Date, Place	Summary of Events and Information	Remarks and References to Appendices
1916.		Strength:- Off. O.R.
H.Q. April 1st 1916	Bat: Billets. H.Q.	Act. Str. 29 - 935
" 2nd		For Rations 17 - 666
" 3rd	Relieved 6th Sherwood Foresters in trenches.	
" 4th	In trenches.	Casualties:-
" 5th	Enemy exploded mine opposite ALBANY at 6.15pm.	Off. O.R.
	Near lip of crater was occupied and consolidated	Killed - 1
	without opposition.	Wounded - 12
" 6th	In trenches.	Total - 13
" 8th		
" 9th	Relieved by 6th S.L.I. and moved back to	
	billets at H.Q.	
" 10th		
" 16th	Bat: billets at H.Q.	
" 17th	Relieved 6th S. Foresters in trenches.	

Army Form C. 2118.

WAR DIARY
INTELLIGENCE SUMMARY.
(Erase heading not required.)

of 8th The Sherwood Foresters

Instructions regarding War Diaries and Intelligence Summaries are contained in F. S. Regs., Part II. and the Staff Manual respectively. Title pages will be prepared in manuscript.

Hour, Date, Place	Summary of Events and Information	Remarks and References to Appendices
April 18th 1916	In trenches - No.2619. Sergt. H.J. SPACEY. "D" Coy. received D.C.M. - No.3192. Corpl W.H. CONERY " 2420. Corpl. A. HARDY. Military Medal for gallantry in recovering men's graves in "No Man's Land" when under heavy enemy fire.	Casualties - Killed Off. O.R. Wounded - - 2 Total - - 2 Strength R. 26.4.16 Bat. Str. Off. 31. O.R. 956 For Trenches 23 761 Reinforcements - Officers. 3 Other ranks - 10th - 41 — 16th - 13/4 - 9 — 18th - 23/4 - 18 —— 68 —— % of men evacuable during month = 3½
" 19th	In trenches	
" 20th	Relieved by 8th Loyal N. Lancs - Moved back to H.Q. at HAROEVILLE. 2 Coys BOIS des ALLEUX, 1 Coy. ECOIVRES, 1 Coy ANZIN.	
" 21st	In billets	
" 22nd " 6th " 28th	} Battalion working on Corps line.	
" 29th	Relieved by 5th Lincolnshire Regt. Embussed at ECOIVRES for AUXI-le-CHATEAU	
" 30th	Attached Battalion to Third Army School.	

J. D. Wilson
Lieut. Col.
C.O. 8th The Sherwood Foresters

1/5 Nott Derby
1C/13

A.13

Army Form C. 2118.

WAR DIARY
INTELLIGENCE SUMMARY.
(Erase heading not required.)

5th Battalion The Sherwood Foresters

Hour, Date, Place	Summary of Events and Information	Remarks and References to Appendices
AUX-LE-CHATEAU		
May 1st 1916	Attached Battalion to Third Army School Aux-le-Chateau	STRENGTH:- Off. O.R.
6. 9.		Total 32 943) 3rd/4/16
10.	Marched to Doullens. 129 Details left at Third Army School	For Duties 24 739)
11.	Marched to Souastre, and joined 139th Infantry Brigade.	Total 35 936) 8th May
12.	Battalion employed finding working parties for French	For Duties 23 714)
6.18.	Cavalry & burying cable, etc. Also course of Instruction in	Reinforcements:-
	Bayonet Fighting.	3 Off. 68 O.R.
19.	Relieved the 5th Batt Staffordshire Regiment in the Right	Casualties:-
	Sector trenches - E27d & K3b (Map Ref. 57D. NE (1:2) 1/20000)	Off. O.R.
20.)		Killed - 1
6.)	In Trenches.	Wounded - 10
31.)		(6 of whom remained at duty)
		Sick evacuation Div. Recd. -
		40 Other ranks -

S.S. Wilson
Lieut. Col.
cdg 5th The Sherwood Foresters

Mr Cordery. 1/f N+D
 June 1916

Please I.A. with
diary.

PRW
18/6/29.

Army Form C. 2118.

WAR DIARY
INTELLIGENCE SUMMARY
(Erase heading not required.)

1/5 Notts & Derby

VC 14

Hour, Date, Place	Summary of Events and Information	Remarks and references to Appendices
FONQUEVILLERS June 1st 1916 3. 2. 6. 16	In trenches	STRENGTH 1.6.16 Off 35 Off 708 Batt. Rankers 25
4th		
5th	Relieved by 5th Batt. Leicestershire Regt. Moved into billets at SOUASTRE.	
	Provided parties for carrying cable & completing new finished portions of STAFFORD AVENUE and ROTTEN ROW	
6th	Relieved by 1/5th Batt. SOUTH STAFFS. at 10.10pm. Battalion marched to LUCHEUX	
7th	Arrive LUCHEUX 2.45am	
8.6.6 17..	Battalion training for the "Push". Bayonet fighting, Physical training, rapid aiming, extended order, also engaged in tree cutting.	
18th	Marches from LUCHEUX to POMMIER	
19th 6 26..	Battalion employed carrying cables, deepening trenches, breaking trench Mortars emplacements. Pumping & carrying fatigues.	

Army Form C. 2118.

WAR DIARY
or
INTELLIGENCE SUMMARY.
(Erase heading not required.)

Instructions regarding War Diaries and Intelligence Summaries are contained in F. S. Regs., Part II. and the Staff Manual respectively. Title pages will be prepared in manuscript.

Hour, Date, Place	Summary of Events and Information	Remarks and references to Appendices
June 27th 1916	Battalion take over the Z␣␣␣␣ line from STAFFORD AVENUE (incl.) to REGENT St (excl.) from 8th Sherwood Foresters.	STRENGTH 24.6.16 OR OFF Battn 37 931 Transers 28 732
28th "	Preparing for the attack — carrying stores up to 6th Sherwood Bumps. Operation postponed. Relieved by 6th Batt. S. Foresters, and moved back into billets a.c. POMMIER.	CASUALTIES 250 OR Killed in action — 2 Wounded — 7 } 13 " (at duty) — 1
29th "	Billets.	SICK evacuated from DIVNL AREA = 18 OR
30th "	Battalion move up to FONQUEVILLERS to take up positions for the attack & relieve 6th Battn Sherwood Foresters in the front line & advanced trenches.	REINFORCEMENTS 5 Off x 22 OR Joined during Month

B. H. Checkland
Major
Comdg 5th Bn The Sherwood Foresters

Army Form C. 2118.

WAR DIARY
or
INTELLIGENCE SUMMARY.
(Erase heading not required.)

Instructions regarding War Diaries and Intelligence Summaries are contained in F. S. Regs., Part II. and the Staff Manual respectively. Title pages will be prepared in manuscript.

Hour, Date, Place	Summary of Events and Information	Remarks and references to Appendices
	Unit 5th Sherwood Foresters. Brigade. Notts & Derby Division North Midland Mobilization Centre. Derby Temporary Var Station Derby Station since occupied subsequent to concentration Luton Harpenden (a) Mobilization (b) Concentration at War Station (including Railway moves) (c) Organization for Defence (including vulnerable points). (d) Training :- After 3 months of mobilization, great improvement is noticed in the bearing of the Battn. My Battalion is now able to march 15 miles in marching order without undue fatigue. (e) Discipline. Improvement is noticed in control exercised by Junior N.C.Os and interior economy has improved. It is certainly more difficult to enforce good discipline when troops are in billets, than when they are in barracks or camp.	

5th Battn. Notts & Derbyshire Regt.
R. Wood Cap/ & Col.
ly. Lieut. Col.

WAR DIARY
or
INTELLIGENCE SUMMARY.
(Erase heading not required.)

Army Form C. 2118.

5th Battn. Notts & Derbyshire Regt.
Lieut. Col.

Hour, Date, Place	Summary of Events and Information	Remarks and references to Appendices
	(1) Administration:- 1. Medical Service. 2. Veterinary Service. 3. Supply Services:- More variation is recommended in rations. After application cocoa is not yet obtainable. 4. Transport Services:- The supply of improvised baker carts wagons on mobilization has caused expense on the substitution of regulation wagons and carts by reason of the harness having to be altered. 5. Ordnance Services. 6. Billeting & Hutting:- Billeting troops in private houses necessarily scatters them over a large area, and causes great loss of time in getting them together. Large rooms or sheds well lighted — in which lectures could be given on winter evenings are required. 7. Channel of correspondence. 8. Range Construction. 9. Supply of Remounts. (2) Reorganization of T.F. Units into Home & Imperial Service. Preparation of Units for Imperial Service.	

Statement in connection with the War diary.

Unit   5th Notts and Derbyshire Regt
Brigade Notts and Derby Infantry Brigade
Division North Midland Division
Mobilization Centre.   Derby
Temporary War Station,   Derby
Stations occupied subsequent to concentration
  (1) Luton
  (2) Harpenden

(a) Mobilization

If mobilization should occur again in the future during the training period whilst the battalion is in camp; its working would be facilitated if the mobilization be completed at camp before the battalion returns to War Station.

(b) Concentration at War Station.

(c) Organization for defence.
        No remarks

(d) Training
1. Great difficulty has been experienced in finding men capable of looking after horses. Suggested that each unit in peace time should include 40 to 50 grooms on its establishment.
2. Further inducements might be given to raise the standard of musketry in peace time. A larger supply of practise ammunition should be at the disposal of units on mobilization.
3. The establishment of eight regular Colour Sergts should be included in the peace establishment in addition to the sergeant major whose pay should be sufficient to attract good men.

(e) Discipline   No remarks.

(f) Administration
Supply service. Suggested that a greater variety of food be provided.
Clothing. A higher standard should be maintained in time of peace. Two good suits of service dress should be held for each man. One pr of ammunition army boots should be given each man annually.

Statement continued

Transport services

Suitable carts including water carts should either be held during peace or earmarked for each unit.

Unsuitable carts are still in possession of this unit two months after mobilization although reported.

Panniers for carrying tools on pack saddles should be provided.

Billeting.
The conditions and terms of billeting should be clearly laid down so that all civilians should understand them.

C.O.s of units should have a contingent fund provided with which to pay the cost of erecting latrines, washing & cooking places, laying on water and otherwise adapting billets.

(g) Reorganisation of T.F. into home and Imperial Service.

No remarks

(h) Preparation of units for imperial service. Advisable that imperial service units be armed with the same rifle as the regular forces.

G. Inseley
Lt Col.
5th Bn North Staffordshire Regt

When marking up documents for copying please tick the appropriate box.

☐ Right hand page only

☐ Left hand page only

☐ Right hand page start

☐ Left hand page start

☐ Right hand page stop

☐ Left hand page stop

Please use a separate slip for each instruction.

e.g. If copying several continuous pages you require one slip to indicate where to start copying and another slip to indicate where the copying should end.

✓ WHEN MARKING UP DOCUMENTS FOR COPYING PLEASE TICK THE APPROPRIATE BOX ON THE OPPOSITE SIDE OF THIS MARKER. THIS INFORMATION IS ESSENTIAL TO ALLOW US TO PROVIDE YOU WITH THE COPIES YOU REQUIRE INFORMATION SHEETS ARE AVAILABLE FROM THE RECORD COPYING COUNTER SHOULD YOU NEED FURTHER ASSISTANCE. ******************************

COPY.

1st JULY 1916 (46th DIVISION).

These Notes were written by T.F.C. Downman, June 1918.

-x-x-x-x-x-

I was posted to "A" Coy & was put in charge of No. 3 Platoon.

I joined the 5th Bn. Sherwood Foresters, the 139th Brigade, 46th Division, VIII Corps, Third Army, on 12th June 1916, the Battalion then being at Lucheaux near Doullens. That day and each day that week the attack was practised over ground supposed to resemble that which would be the scene of the real action. These practices were continually begun, stopped and sent back and recommenced. Equipment was altered several times and generally put into a state of muddle.

18th June the Battalion marched to Pommier and took up billets there, from here working parties went up to the front every day. Occasional shelling of the village especially after the batteries of 9.2's had commenced their work. The evening of the 27th the Battalion went into the trenches in support, the attack being timed for 7.30 a.m. on 29th. The trenches were deep in mud and lacking duck boards; this deficiency was begun to be made good on morning of 28th. The evening 28th the Battalion moved out of the trenches back to Pommier. The attack was withheld for 48 hours, thereby losing the value of the artillery preparation, enabling the enemy to organize his defences, and spoiling the spirit of our men.

We had already had elaborate instructions as to what to do when we had reached our objectives, and instructions as to flares, Verey lights, and numerous other details. So there being nothing further to learn (?) we spent a quiet time till the afternoon of the 30th June. That evening we moved up to the trenches and again had parties carrying duck boards. My platoon had already been reduced from a strength of 35 to 20, fifteen men being taken as bombers, runners, carriers &c., then during the board carrying a shell wounded my platoon sergeant and 4 men of my platoon, reducing the strength to 15.

At 11 p.m. we moved up to the front line going over the top for some distance. We eventually reached our portion of the line (3 bays for 1 platoon), about midnight. From about 12 to 12.30 a.m. 1st July the enemy machine guns were very active, just passing over the parapet of our front line. After this had died down I sent a small party out, about six men who each had wire cutters, to clear the path through our wire; this was soon done and I went out myself right through the gap which was quite well cleared. I attempted to report to my Company Commander who was with Battalion headquarters, but lost my way down a badly battered communication trench (I had only been down this once before and that was in daylight and before the Bosch had bombarded it. All our communication trenches were in good condition a week before the attack, but had been systematically bombarded by the Bosch during the last few days). I regained the front line and sat on the firing step until daylight; during this time the trenches were shelled by the enemy with small high explosives. About 3.30 a.m. hot tea with rum mixed in came along, I saw this distributed to my platoon, who each had a cupful, and then passed on to the next platoon.

Soon after this casualties came along, chiefly from the Monmouths who had been out digging an advanced line, a dead man was deposited in my middle bay. At 5 a.m. I went into a dugout and remained there ¾ of an hour. I then returned to my station (the next bay) and waited there. An issue of neat rum came round, each man in my platoon had a small cupful.

After the intense bombardment had started at 6.30 a.m. the enemy replied with shrapnel on my right, but nothing came near me. At 7.25 a.m. the platoon on my left (No. 2) were to go out and I was to follow and get behind them (70 yards interval) at 7.28 a.m. I remained to the left of my platoon and in communication with a man of No. 2 platoon, at 7.26 I called to him and asked if No. 2 had gone, he replied NO; again at 7.27, 7.28, 7.29 and 7.30 I received the same reply; as I was then 2 minutes overdue I decided not to wait and immediately gave the order for No. 3 to go over.

Smoke bombs had been thrown out about 7.20 a.m. and did nothing but make a thick fog of evil smelling and tasting smoke on our own parapet, making it difficult to find the way out and calculated to lose one's sense of direction. When beyond the smoke I looked for my platoon which should have been lined up in the prone position in front of our own wire, but I could see no one, either to right, left, or ahead. Looking back I saw a party coming out carrying tremendous burdens, offering a good target and moving very slowly. This was No. 4 platoon, supposed to bring up wire, steel poles, bombs, flares &c for "A" Coy. Without waiting I proceeded towards the German lines alone, taking a direction towards the left, according to instructions. I passed the advanced line, a very shallow and narrow trench and came to a very large shell hole, here I came up with 2 men of my platoon who had evidently gone on without waiting for me. They gave me the direction further to the left and followed me. I was not aware of shells, bullets or other missiles whilst in the open. On reaching the German wire I found it well cut and smashed up and had no difficulty in getting through. On reaching the German front line I found a trench nearly eight feet deep, very wide and apparently totally blocked at one end and partially blocked at the other. It was quite empty. I jumped in and climbed out the other side, still followed by the two men I met in the open, but I do not remember seeing them after this. Between the Bosch 1st and 2nd line I was in the open until noticing a communication trench on my left I jumped into it and was going up when I saw head of me two "chevaux de frises" lying at the bottom of the trench affecting a temporary barricade. When nearing this about half a dozen bullets hit the side of the trench a yard in front of me, evidently a machine gun, but fortunately finished a belt or jambed as I got over the obstacle and proceeded. I soon saw Second Lieut. McInnes of "D" Coy ahead; he called to me to come on evidently thinking I had brought reinforcements. I reached him in the 2nd German line and found it very badly knocked about on the right resembling sand hills, quite irregular; to the left the trench was in

evoking some comment. Several Germans then lined the
fire step and threw a few bombs, there was no reply and
they had retaken this portion of their 2nd line effectually
scattering our little party. Whilst still lying
on the floor of the trench I was threatened with the
bayonet and was nearly finished off by one but fortunately
this was averted. A German then bandaged my arm with
my field dressing and left me to myself. After some
minutes as all the Germans had disappeared I managed to
crawl out into a shallow trench going about 10 yards in
the direction of the 1st line. Here I remained from
8.20 a.m. to 12.30 p.m. during which time our shells were
again active on the 2nd line, several pieces coming very
near to me. At 12.30 I thought it advisable to seek
better cover and crawled back and found the entrance to a
dug-out which I thought was empty. I went down a few
steps and sat down. After 10 minutes or so a German N.C.O.
came along and took me down the dug-out, about 40 feet
deep. Here there were several Germans in a large dug-out
fitted with beds, tables &c. I was given some cold coffee
and my belongings were looked at. My revolver ammunition
alone was taken away. Shelling of these lines was
going on all the time, whilst I was in this dug-out and
a shell burst at the mouth and threw large quantities of
earth down, covering the pack and equipment of a German
who had been neatly arranging them on the steps. About
2.30 p.m. I was taken to another dug-out some distance to
the right and most probably in the 3rd line. This was a
large place with several rooms, bed rooms with ordinary
iron bedsteads, furniture &c. I was placed at a small
table in a passage near an officers' mess. This mess
belonged to the 91st Regiment. Here I was given hot
coffee, kriegsbrot and some sausage meat, also cigarettes.
The Major or Colonel of this regiment was seated at a
large table with all the junior officers around; he
commenced reading a long report to them, in the middle
he turned round and asked me my name; this by the way was
the only question that was asked me. I was not searched
or interrogated. I noticed my very light pistol on the
table. This seemed to be regarded with suspicion, so
I asked an orderly who spoke English if I could speak to
the Colonel. This was quite readily granted, so I
explained that the very light pistol was merely a signal
pistol and not a new pocket trench mortar. This German
officer understood and showed me his store of signal
cartridges, several thousands and of a variety of colours;
they were smaller than ours and looked very much like a
sporting cartridge, of not too large a bore. I also
noticed some of their pistols which had barrels nearly
twice the length of the cartridges, thus accounting for
the superiority of their lights over ours of that date.

About 5.30 p.m. I was sent to a dressing station in
the trenches, on the way I noticed several of our 9.2"
shells lying in the mud at the bottom of the trenches;
if all of these had exploded the results would have been
very useful to us. The dressing station was about 50
feet below the surface and well fitted up with an opera-
ting table equipment and instruments of all kinds. There
were stretchers and beds in various rooms off the passages.
After waiting here some time whilst several Bosch were
attended to, I was bound up and sent upstairs again. Here
I found a string of lightly wounded Bosch and looked
round for the sentry, with rifle, who had brought me there,
expecting to be escorted somewhere. However the sentry
had gone and the wounded bosch made it plain that I was

to join their party. This I had to do being placed second
in the single file. We went down the trenches in this
fashion being followed by English 18-pounders. We had to
wait and go down a dug-out, full of wounded Bosch, for
nearly an hour, then we proceeded still with numerous
shells falling near. I understood from the behaviour
of the Germans and their evident "wind" that another
attack was in progress. However, if there was one it was
soon over and did not get anywhere near us. We proceeded
and went some miles zigzagging about; we passed several
small parties coming up, about 7 or 8 under an officer;
some of them asked me for money, but I took no notice
of these requests. We eventually came to a road and
got out of the trench and went over the open going back
towards some village behind the lines. This area was
swept by spent bullets which whistled through the grass.
On reaching the high road probably that between Bucquoy
and Puisseaux, our party consisted of myself with about
6 bosch wounded; the others, about another dozen wounded,
had evidently dropped out on the way. This road was
being shelled with shrapnel by our field guns. Several
transport carts coming along had narrow escapes but none
were hit. We reached a village about 9 p.m. by my watch.

From my own observations and from information
obtained from officers, N.C.O's and men of the 46th and
56th Divisions I arrive at the following:

Ours was a subsidiary attack and kind of extra to
the main attack further South, but at the same time it
was intended to be successful and to capture the strong
positions made about the Gommecourt Wood.
 The attack failed through various causes of which the
following are the chief:

The absurdly inadequate strength of some of the
attacking units; my own battalion went over between 500
and 600 strong. My own platoon consisted of 15.
 Lack of knowledge on the part of the higher commands
of the conditions prevailing in the trenches and of what
was likely to take place in an attack on trenches from
trenches.
 The absurd distribution of equipment: those in 1st
waves who got into the German lines having to wait for
4th waves who never got there.
 Overloading of all attackers, especially "carriers".
 Very bad management regarding cutting of German
barbed wire; this was absolutely uncut on a 2 battalion
front, letting down our right flank and the 56th Division's
left flank. The wire on my own front was sufficiently cut
owing to the energies of Lt. Lilley who had taken patrols
out to do this work, the artillery not being sufficiently
competent to do it properly.
 Half-heartedness in regard to the attack by Divisional
General (46th Division). Only 4 battalions went into
attack at 7.30 a.m. They were not supported and no
reinforcements were sent. I understand that subsequent
attacks by the rest of the division took place during the
day, none of which reached the German lines. If these
troops had all attacked between 7.30 and 8 a.m. we should
have gained our objectives and held them, presuming that
the wire was cut.

-x-x-x-x-

WAR DIARY
INTELLIGENCE SUMMARY

Army Form C. 2118.

July 1916
15 Notts & Derby 139
46

Vol 15

H.15

Hour, Date, Place	Summary of Events and Information	Remarks and References to Appendices
FONQUEVILLERS July 1, 1916.	46th Division's attack at GOMMECOURT. Two Brigades assaulting (137th & 139th), Two Battalions (5th & 7th) found first three waves of the assault of the 139th Brigade in support, & the 8th in reserve. The objective of this Battalion was the German 3rd front line north edge of GOMMECOURT WOOD on the right, & a point 250 yards north west of MOCO C.T. crossed the 3rd river. Companies were organised in four waves, the rear Platoon of wave carrying bombs & material for consolidation. D. Company was on the right – A. Company in the centre & C. Company on the left – "B" Company was detailed to do the carrying. The final Bombardment began at 6.25 a.m. Smoke bombs were thrown at 7.25 & the first three waves moved to the assault from three minutes later. The enemy set up a triple barrage of artillery & trench Mortar fire & concentrated upon the Battalion front	STRENGTH - 5.7.16 Officers 26 Or Ranks 562 For Duties 1/2 401

K French Notes   Forms/C. 2118/10.

WAR DIARY or INTELLIGENCE SUMMARY

Army Form C. 2118.

Hour, Date, Place	Summary of Events and Information	Remarks and References to Appendices
July 1.	cont^d from very heavy machine gun fire. The first three waves attacked with great dash & many are known to have reached the enemy's first trench, but casualties during the advance were very heavy & the enemy opposition was well organised. The fourth waves were delayed by their heavy losses & by the muddy state of the trenches over the heavy rains - They moved over the parapet 15 minutes late. The carrying company was delayed still more for similar reasons, & advanced at 8.10. a.m. By this time the smoke had to a great extent cleared & the enemy seeing troops forming on accurate & withering fire - completely checking further advance. From Aeroplane observation it is thought some men reached & for a time held part of the enemy's second system, but it was not possible to send up support, & owing to failure to reach their objective Part of the Brigade on the right & reach their objective	

Army Form C. 2118.

WAR DIARY
or
INTELLIGENCE SUMMARY.
(Erase heading not required.)

Hour, Date, Place	Summary of Events and Information	Remarks and References to Appendices
July 1	contd. The right flank of the Battalion was exposed. Efforts were made later in the day to send fresh troops to the assault but these were without success. The attack succeeded in its object to the extent that enough troops were held in front of the German to have altered the whole course of the Battalions further south. The Battalion was relieved at 7 pm & moved into billets at BIENVILLERS.	After this attack Lt. Col. D.G. Wilson was reported missing & Major B.A. Chicksland assumed command of the Battalion. REINFORCEMENTS:- OR 422 ——— EVACUATED Dont. Aus. 22
July 2	Moved at 5 pm to billets at WARLINCOURT.	
July 3	Moved at 11 a.m to billets at SAULTY.	
July 4, 5, 6		
July 7		
July 8	Major General the Hon. E. Montagu-Stuart-Worthy C.B., C.M.G., M.V.O., D.S.O. said good bye to the senior officers of the Brigade. Inspection by the new G.O.C. Major General W. Thwaites.	
July 10	Moved to BELLACOURT relieving 5th Batt. Kings Own Royal Lancs. Regiment in Brigade Reserve.	

Army Form C. 2118.

WAR DIARY
or
INTELLIGENCE SUMMARY.
(Erase heading not required.)

Instructions regarding War Diaries and Intelligence Summaries are contained in F. S. Regs, Part II. and the Staff Manual respectively. Title pages will be prepared in manuscript.

Hour, Date, Place	Summary of Events and Information	Remarks and References to Appendices
July 1 to 15.	In Brigade Reserve at BELLACOURT	CASUALTIES:-
July 16	Relieved 6th Sherwood Foresters in right sector trenches	Missing O.R. 16 / 194
		Killed in action 3 / 80
July 20	B. A. & D Companies on the line. "C" Company in support	Wounded 1 / 222
	Enemy in the early morning heavily bombarded the front line trenches on sector occupied by "A" Company	
July 23	Relieved by 6th Sherwood Foresters & moved into Divisional Reserve at BAILLEULVAL	STRENGTH:- O.R.
July 29	Relieved the 6th Sherwood Foresters in right sector trenches - "B" "C" & "D" Companies on the line, "A" Company in support	Relief 23 / 740
		Trenches 17 / 614
July 30 & 31	Company in support in trenches -	

W H Checkland
Major
Commanding 5th Sherwood Foresters

To Headquarters,

    139th Infantry Brigade.

    ———————

    Herewith 5th Battalion The Sherwood Foresters War Diary for the month of August, 1916.

B H Checkland.
    Lieut. Col.,
    cdg. 5th The Sherwood Foresters.

3/9/16.

WAR DIARY
INTELLIGENCE SUMMARY

Army Form C. 2118.

5*th* The Sherwood Foresters.

Vol 16

Hour, Date, Place 1916.	Summary of Events and Information	Remarks and References to Appendices
BELLACOURT		
August 1*st* 1916	In Trenches X.2.c.10.50 & X.3.G.5.4	Strength
to 4*th* "		Off 23 O.R.
" 5*th* "	Brigade Reserve in BELLACOURT	Batt'n 16 870
to 10*th* "		Trenches 606
" 11*th* "	In Trenches	
to 16*th* "		Casualties during Month
" 17*th* "	Battalion moved back into Divisional Reserve in billets at BAILLEULVAL	Killed in action -- 1
to 21*st* "		Wounded -do- -- 4
" 22*nd* "	Relieved 6*th* Batt Sherwood Foresters in trenches	(including) -- 5
" 23*rd* "	In Trenches	*Officer slightly wounded remained at duty
" 24*th* "		
	2*nd* Lieut SANDOVER and 14 O.R. attempted unsuccessful raid on the enemy trenches at Point X.2.C. 47.37 (M36)	Reinforcements
	Ref 57C & 51B SW 1/10000	23 Officers 86 other ranks
" 25*th* "	In Trenches	Sick evacuated
" 28*th* "		1 Off 14 other ranks
" 29*th* "	In Brigade Reserve in BELLACOURT	
to 31*st* "		Strength
		Off O.R.
		Batt'n 46 916
		Trenches 33 628

M.H. Muirhead Lieut Col.
C.dg. 5*th* The Sherwood Foresters.

Army Form C. 2118.

WAR DIARY
or
INTELLIGENCE SUMMARY
(Erase heading not required.)

5:12 of the Lenwood Foresters

Instructions regarding War Diaries and Intelligence Summaries are contained in F. S. Regs., Part II. and the Staff Manual respectively. Title pages will be prepared in manuscript.

Hour, Date, Place	Summary of Events and Information	Remarks and References to Appendices
BELLACOURT. Sept 1st and 2nd 1916	In Brigade Reserve at BELLACOURT (R31). "C" Company in support trenches.	Map FICHEUX - Sh S.E and 5I S.S.W.
3rd/16	Between 6th Batt Lenwood Foresters in Brigade	Strength Offr 42 O.R. 915
4th/16 5th/16	Brigade Relief Trenches (X.1.a. & R.32.a). In trenches	Offr 44 915 In trenches O.R. 620
8th/16	Patrol under Lieut SMALLEY and Lieut CLARK attempted to cut gaps in enemy wire at X.1.a.55.10 and X.2.6.61.51 with view of Removal each 25 × long, and afterwards raid the enemy trench. Lieut SMALLEY in fact successfully entered the line but when attempting to get through the wire found he had about 12 yards and had not been cut and consequently no rush could Lieut CLARKS' party came up against a strong enemy working and covering party in front of his BLOCKHOUSE and could not approach his objective.	REINFORCEMENTS 1 Officer × 46 O.R. ═══ ═══ SICK Other ranks evacuated during month — 18 4 officers struck off
9th/16	Relieved by 1st Battalion Sherwood Foresters and moved back into Divisional Reserve in huts at BAILLEUL VAL (W.5.a)	═══
10th/16 11th/16	Battalion engaged carrying 900 cylinders to front line trenches.	
12th " 13th " 14th "	In Reserve	

WAR DIARY

INTELLIGENCE SUMMARY.

5th Bn. Sherwood Foresters

Hour, Date, Place	Summary of Events and Information	Remarks and References to Appendices
September 15th/1916	Relieved 6th Battalion Sherwood Foresters in Right Sector trenches.	CASUALTIES:-
16/16 to 18/16	In trenches.	Killed 2 O.R.
19"	Parties under Lieut W. Donegan and 2/Lieut T. Hutchinson attacked 2 small gaps in enemy's wire at X.1.a.0.10 and raid enemy Bps. at points X.1.a.74.52 and X.2.c.20.70. Lieut W. Donegan's party was unable to get through the wire after repeatedly efforts to do so. 2/Lieut T. Hutchinson's party successfully entered the Bp. but were unable to enter the enemy Bp.	Wounded Offr. 1 (remained at duty) O.R. 9 (1 remained at duty)
20"	Relieved by 6th Battalion Sherwood Foresters and moved back into Brigade Reserve at BELLACOURT. "A" Coy on the posts. "D" Coy attached to 6th Bn. as front line Coy. "B" Coy. at BRETENCOURT.	
21"/16 to 24"	Brigade Reserve.	
25"	Relieved 6th Battalion S.F. in Right Sector trenches.	
26" to 29"	In trenches.	

Army Form C. 2118.

WAR DIARY (3)
INTELLIGENCE SUMMARY.
(Erase heading not required.)

5ᵗʰ The Hertford Loreto

Hour, Date, Place	Summary of Events and Information	Remarks and References to Appendices
September 30 2/16	A party under 2/Lt PATTINSON attempted to blow a gap in the enemy wire at X.1.a.01.10, and afterward raid the enemy trench at Point X.1.a.0.12. He at hide of movement was placed in the enemy wire at 9.30.pm. but, believing to be sight of a German flare that the wire was not in the reg'd place, 2/Lt PATTINSON withdrew it and again moved it cautiously under cover the enemy were anything into showing grenades. He then was exploded successfully and the party attacked the wire, but were bombed back by a party of five Germans in the wire. 2/Lt PATTINSON and 1 men being slightly wounded. Our party was hales the gap for 10 or 15 minutes - 3 of our bombs having been seen to explode near 3 Germans who had got up to fire & who were not seen again.	STRENGTH. off O.R. Total 43 903 For trenches 26 631

K.A. Uhckland Lieut Col,
C'dg 5ᵗʰ The Hertford Loreto

October 1916 Vol 15

Army Form C. 2118.

1/5th Bn. The Sherwood Foresters

WAR DIARY
INTELLIGENCE SUMMARY
(Erase heading not required.)

Instructions regarding War Diaries and Intelligence Summaries are contained in F. S. Regs., Part II. and the Staff Manual respectively. Title pages will be prepared in manuscript.

Hour, Date, Place	Summary of Events and Information	Remarks and References to Appendices
Trenches GROMMELLE		Strength 1-10-16
October 1st 1916	Relieved by 6th Batt. Sherwood Foresters and marched back into Divisional Reserve BARLEUX-VAL	Off 29 OR 891
2am	Battalion re-arrived with R.E. & c.	Batt in trenches 843
3am	employed carrying the garrison	5 in trenches 24
4th	Battalion in reserve at garrison. The Battalion	Casualties killed wounded
5th	"	Officers - 2
6th	by M. Gen. THWAITES G.O.C. Division	Rank & file 4 7
7th	" billets in reserve	2 in draft
8th	Relieved 6th Batt. in trenches	
12th	In trenches	Evacuated
13th	Relieved by 6th Battalion and moved into Brigade Reserve	1 off 30 OR 76
14th	in Brigade Reserve BELLACOURT	
18th	In billets in reserve	Reinforcements
19th	Relieved 6th Battalion in Trenches	37 Other Ranks
20th	"	
21st	"	
22nd	"	Strength 28/10/16
26th	Relieved by 6th Battalion & moved into Div. Reserve BARLEUX-VAL	Officers 28/10/16
27th	Battalion inspected by His Grace the Duke of Devonshire	Off 27
28th		OR 909
29th	Training	631
30th	Battalion relieved 1st 10th Household Bn & in trenches 6	
31st	Sir St. LEGER &	
	Ht. Sir St. LEGER.	

A.M. Hughes Major
Cdg 5th Bn The Sherwood Foresters

WAR DIARY — November, 1916 —

Vol 19

5th Battalion The Sherwood Foresters

Army Form C. 2118.

INTELLIGENCE SUMMARY.
(Erase heading not required.)

Instructions regarding War Diaries and Intelligence Summaries are contained in F. S. Regs., Part II. and the Staff Manual respectively. Title pages will be prepared in manuscript.

Hour, Date, Place	Summary of Events and Information	Remarks and References to Appendices
Les. St. LEGER.		Receipts
November 1st 1916.	Marched to new billets at BARLY.	O.R.
2nd "		Batt. 37 891
3rd "	Marched to new billets at ONEUX.	Drafts 27 719
4th–6th "		
6th–20th "	Battalion training:— Gas warfare; Night & Raiding	Casualties
21st "	formations; Assaults on & from trenches; Musketry; Bomb	Nil
22nd "	Company & Extd order drill; Physical training.	
23rd "	Marched to DOMLEGER.	Reinforcements
24th "	Marched to BARLY.	2 off. 27 O.R.
25th "		
26th "	Marched to Les. St. LEGER.	Evacuates
–6th "		23
30th "	Les. St. LEGER.	
		Strength
		O.R.
		Batt. 36 896
		Drafts 28 702

M Taylor
Lieut. Col.
Cdg. 5th The Sherwood Foresters

To Headquarters,
    139th Infantry Brigade.
    _____

            Herewith WAR DIARY for
Month ending 31st December, 1916.

                                    [signature]
                                            Major,
            cdg. 5th The Sherwood Foresters.

3/1/17.

5th The Sherwood Foresters

Vol 20

Army Form C. 2118.

WAR DIARY
INTELLIGENCE SUMMARY.
December/916 – 5th Sherwoods.
(Erase heading not required.)

Instructions regarding War Diaries and Intelligence Summaries are contained in F. S. Regs, Part II. and the Staff Manual respectively. Title pages will be prepared in manuscript.

Hour, Date, Place	Summary of Events and Information	Remarks and References to Appendices
Fos. St- LEGER –		STRENGTH 30/11/16
December 1st	In billets – Bde Ceremonial Inspn.	Base 36 Off 828 O.R.
2nd	Inspection by G.O.C. Division.	Trench 28 702
3rd	Church Parade	REINFORCEMENTS:
4th	Marched to new sector at SOUASTRE.	2 Off 9R O.B.
5th	Relieved 4th Batt Riding in trenches K3c.3.6.6 & K28.c.2.6	CASUALTIES
	(Map – FONQUEVILLERS (1/40,000)) Xt Salvador.	Killed – – 3 O.R.
6th, 6th }	In trenches	Wounded – – 7 ,
11th }		– do – (at duty) – 1½ ,
12th	Relieved by 6th Sherwood Foresters & moved into Bde Support – H.Q. –	EVACUATED
	2. Coys at FONQUEVRE & 2 Coys in Rising Points in FONQUEVILLERS.	1 Off 37 O.R.
13th, 14th }	In Bde Support. Battalion engaged on various fatigues: work.	STRENGTH 28/12/16
17th }	Such notes hr & cleaning trenches. O.C. Major Capron 6th	BATTN 37 Off 924 O.R.
18th	N Staffs assumed command of Battalion 15/12/16.	TRENCH 20 , 602 ,
19th	Relieved 6th Batt in Xt Salvador.	
19th, 6th }	In trenches – During enemy raid on trenches of our Bn – Bdes	
21st }	(425) on 19th he hardly bombarded our Bde front for about	
	2 hrs commencing at 8.30 pm. Enemy commenced barrage 6	
	am trenches & inflicting considerable casualties.	
22nd	Returned by 6th S.F. & moved into Divr Reserve at SOUASTRE.	
23rd, 24th }	In Divisional Reserve	
25th }		
26th	Rem 6th S.F. in Xt Salvador.	
27th, }		
28th }	In trenches	
29th }		
30th	Relvd by 6th S.F. & moved into Bde Support	
31st	In Brigade Support	
	The cases of Trench Feet during this month –	

John Hey Major.
Cdg 5th The Sherwood Foresters –

H 20

WAR DIARY
INTELLIGENCE SUMMARY

1/5 Notts & Derby Regt
Army Form C. 2118
January, 1917

Hour, Date, Place	Summary of Events and Information	Remarks and references to Appendices
FOUFFLES		
January 1917		
1st / 2nd	To Brigade Reserve. 2 Coys in FONQUEVILLERS, remainder of Battalion in SOUASTRE	Strength O.R.
		Off 35 907
3rd	Relieved 6th S.F. in Kt. Catapult	16 576
4th / 6th	At Kinesco.	
7th	Relieved by 6th S.F. & moved back into Divisional Reserve at SOUASTRE	Casualties O.R.
		Off — 2
8th	Capt. HARRISON and Lieut. BRUCE - PETTIGREW & 25 O.R. formed part of Guard of Honour to 3rd Army Commander on decoration parade at Divl. H.Q.	" (Accidental) — 3
		Died in hos — 1
9th / 10th	In Divl. Reserve.	
11th	Relieved 6th Sher. Fors. in Kt. Labrador	Reinforcements O.R.
12th	In trenches.	Off — 5 67
13th	Some Stokes mortar cuts on the enemy wire opposite our Battalion front. 12 O.R. & 1 Officer - 2 Ammunite Parties & each 2 Officers buried at Stokes & exploded 150 & taken at ZERO Hours (9.5pm) and are in Parties returned to our lines without casualties by 9.26 pm. Any one retaliation on the part of the enemy.	Evacuations Off — 2 O.R. 30
14th	In trenches.	
15th	Relieved by 6th C.F.F. & moved into Bde Reserve - 2 Coys in FONQUEVILLERS as remainder of Battalion in SOUASTRE	
16th / 18th	In Brigade Reserve	
19th	Relieved 6th S.F. in Kt. Labrador	

WAR DIARY
or
INTELLIGENCE SUMMARY. January. 1917.
(Erase heading not required.)

Army Form C. 2118.

Hour, Date, Place	Summary of Events and Information	Remarks and references to Appendices
1917		
January		
20th 21st 22nd	In trenches	
23rd	Relieved by 6th S.F & moved back into Divisional Reserve in Bivouacs.	
24th 25th 26th	In Divisional Reserve.	
27th	Relieved 6th S.F. in X.1. Subsector.	Strength Off. O.Rs Batt. 37. 925. Trench 18. 526
28th 29th 30th	In trenches.	
31st	Relieved by 6th Sherwood Foresters and moved back into Brigade Reserve	

C.L. Ashwell. Major.

c.o.g. 5th The Sherwood Foresters

To Headquarters,
    139th Infantry Brigade.
    ─────────────────

        Herewith War Diary of my Battalion
for the month of February, 1917.

                        B.H. Checkland. Lieut. Col.,
                        cdg. 5th The Sherwood Foresters.

3rd Mar/17.

FEBRUARY 1917

H.22

Army Form C. 2118.

WAR DIARY
INTELLIGENCE SUMMARY.
(Erase heading not required.)

Vol 22
1/5th The Sherwood Foresters

Instructions regarding War Diaries and Intelligence Summaries are contained in F. S. Regs., Part II. and the Staff Manual respectively. Title pages will be prepared in manuscript.

Hour, Date, Place	Summary of Events and Information	Remarks and References to Appendices
OUATRE –		STRENGTH
February 1st 1917	The Brigade Brown. 2 Coys in OUATRE and 2 Coys in EUGENBUSQUE	Off 0.76
2nd "		Battalion 37 923
3rd "		Trench 18 526
4th "	Relieved 6th R.C. Scots at Ft. Lambton trenches. Hd Qrs & Coy of 7/S.F.	
5th "	Lorraine B/ft. Brigade attached for instructional purposes.	CASUALTIES
6th "	In trenches	Killed 1.3
7th "		Wounded & at duty 1.8
8th "	Relieved 6th & 7/S. Foresters. B/ft. Brigade & troops into Divisional	" (to hospital) 19.1
9th "	Reserve at SOMERTZ.	
10th "	In huts at Div. Boust.	REINFORCEMENTS:-
11th "	Party of 6 Hallsey for returning	81 other ranks
12th "	Relieved 7/S.L.R.B in V.1 South.	
13th "	In trenches. Hd Qrs were 1 Coy & 2/Wilkinson.	EVACUATED Sick others 15 other ranks
14th "	2nd Lt F.H. Warwick were party entered the Enemy trenches at the Point and penetrated to 2nd German line. No enemy encountered.	
15th "	Relieved by 7/6" L.R.B and moved back into Divisional Reserve. "A" Coy refining Battalion.	
16th "	Divisional Reserve in huts.	
17th "	Relieved 2/5" L.R.B in V.1 South.	
18th "	In trenches.	
19th "	Relieved by 4" Leicestershire & moved back into huts at St AMAND.	
20th "	Marched to Sous-le-Leger. Lt Col J.H. CHECKLAND rejoined & resumed Command.	
21st "	from ENGLAND and resumed Command.	
	Rt K.P.	

(Continued)

FEBRUARY 1917 WAR DIARY 2
or (continued)
INTELLIGENCE SUMMARY.

1/5 2nd The Seaforth Forsters

Army Form C. 2118.

Hour, Date, Place	Summary of Events and Information	Remarks and References to Appendices
February 22nd 1917	In billets at Bus F. LEGER. Brigade exercise. Zaining. Bugging Kirchen of Stoning Road.	STRENGTH Off 0.R Brew 37 934 Indus 26 605
23		
24		
25		
26		
27		
28	Battalion ordered to march to meet trench train SAPIGNCOURT. Order cancelled. Battalion marched to HARBOY.	

M.M. Checkland Lieut Col.
comdg 5" The Seaforth Forsters

1/5 Nott'd R
March 1917
H-23

Army Form C. 2118.

WAR DIARY
or
INTELLIGENCE SUMMARY.
(Erase heading not required.)

Instructions regarding War Diaries and Intelligence Summaries are contained in F. S. Regs., Part II. and the Staff Manual respectively. Title pages will be prepared in manuscript.

ORDERLY ROOM 5TH SHERWOOD FORESTERS

Hour, Date, Place	Summary of Events and Information	Remarks and References to Appendices
March 1st	In billets at ST AMAND.	MAP - 57 D NE - 1/20,000
		STRENGTH -
		Off. O.R.
		Total 37 968
		For trenches 23 651
2nd	Attacked 6. 139th Inf. Bde - Relieved 4th Leicesters at 9 a.m. "A" Company in front trench S. of LA BRAYELLE RD - 2 Platoons of "B" Coy attached 460. Field Coy for work - "C" Coy at support of 6th & "D" Coy be carrying parties - "D" Coy in support. Rations "B" & "D" Coys were attached to 5th Leicesters & reported to their H.Q. in GOMMECOURT WOOD. Dugout on 2nd. 139th Inf. Bde relieved 138th Inf. Bde in GOMMECOURT SECT.	
3rd		
4th	5th Battalion moved forward & took over right subsection from K6.c.3.2 to RADFAHRER GRABEN. Dispositions were "D" & "D" Coys in front. GOMMECOURT about K.1.c.6.3 - 18th? Durham 9th Infantry Brigade on right - 8th Batt. 9th on left. "A" Coy was relieved by 1st Batt. M.F. before moving up in support. During the day enemy retired to a line East of B152 WOOD. "D" Coy in support.	Reinforcements
	ROTTEMOY FARM. Patrols were pushed forward to B152 WOOD and ROTTEMOY FARM during the night.	2 Off. 85. O.R.
5th	ROTTEMOY FARM was occupied at 5.30 a.m. During the day S.S.I. line was established from S.E. corner of B152 WOOD to K.30.C. 2 Officers & patrols joined "A" & "B" & "D" Companies. "A" Coy in support in GRABE M Crowning line - C Coy in Support in STAFFORD TRENCH - Battalion H.Q. reestablished at K.5.d.6.7. at 11.30 a.m. Rations & water brought up by Pack Transport. Every communication with 139th East Yorks. 92nd Infantry Brigade secured on the night.	Scott Wowalcile Ins. Arr.
6th	8th Batt. S.F. on left relieved by 6th Battalion S.F. Enemy bombarded his own front line at 12.45 a.m. after sending up 3 lots of white Verey Lights from about F.55 & K.7 at 12.30 a.m. "D" Coy (on left) attempted to occupy ROTTEMOY GRABEN but encountered the enemy in force were unable to do so.	27.

(Continued).

Army Form C. 2118.

WAR DIARY (2)
INTELLIGENCE SUMMARY.
(Erase heading not required.)

March, 1917

Hour, Date, Place	Summary of Events and Information	Remarks and References to Appendices
Mar. 6° (cont)	A Coy relieved D. C. relieved B about 5pm. Line unchanged. Patrols active during night.	
7°	Line of defence more consolidated. Enemy movement at 2.30 a.m: about 5.30pm but no serious orch. RETTEMOY GRABEN found to be strongly held by enemy. Patrols prowling during night. Division Reinforced B & C Coys at Noon.	CASUALTIES Killed Off. O.R Off. 2 Wounded 3 60 Wounded of 3 10 (missing)
8°	Patrols sent forward to ascertain position of enemy. He was encountered in force along F.2 c.8.9 and in RETTEMOY GRABEN. During night enemy was found to be strongly holding BUCQUOY GRABEN. In cooperation with an attack by the Battalion on our Right and KANDSTURM GRABEN at F.30 c.10.55. Batt. in RANDSTURM GRABEN withdrawn to F.30 c.10.55. Battalion relieved by 7th Batt. S.F. moved back into Divil Stores. Transport lines at SOUASTRE. Batt. H.Q at BROWERY. Q.14. A. Div. Reserve.	
9° 10°		
11°	Relieved 7th Battalion L.F. who attacked 1 Coy 6 am on R.S.L. 07. B+C Coys ant. A+D Coys going ant. C Coy in Support. Battalion H.Q at a GOMMECOURT Rd. Shelled with various calibres + gas shells during FONQUEVILLERS relief during night.	
12°	B Coy moved making strong forms on PIGEON TRENCH & form second line of defence. Battalion H.Q. 2 Platoon of B Coy moved up to RETTEMOY FARM at 5pm. by K Capt. Battalion and EWARTS was being evacuated during afternoon. But on Battalion a Patrol was found RETTEMOY GRABEN occupied. One gun was released to HQ night so far no L. 2. 2. 3 with HQ and of another Company from 7th Battalion.	

WAR DIARY (3)

Army Form C. 2118.

— March, 1917 —

Hour, Date, Place	Summary of Events and Information	Remarks and References to Appendices
March 12th (cont'd)	Patrol sent out from BIEZ Wood reports enemy wire between L.2.c.2.6 & F.26.a.0.0. to be broken & unknown. "A" Coy, "D" Coy & 1 platoon of "C" Coy with remaining 3 platoons of "C" Coy as carrying party attacked RETTEMOY GRABEN from F.25.a.2.7 to F.25.a.12.87. Objective was reached — enemy counter attacked with very heavy rifle & MG fire — cannot advance at L.2.c.10.30.	
13th	A & D Coys relieved by B & C Coys. 2 platoons in each Coy front line — BIEZ Wood, front was held by 7th Battalion F.S.	
14th	At 1 am 137th Infantry Bde attacked BUCQUOY GRABEN from our right Battalion front. To co-operate patrols were sent forward to try & obtain entry to BUCQUOY GRABEN to the N of portion attacked. But owing to M.G. rifle & T.M fire they were unable to do so. Wiring & patrolling carried out at night. Bands from LANDSTURM GRABEN along RETTEMOY GRABEN as far as F.25.a.25.85. Quiet night.	
15th	Patrol proceeded to F.25.a.75.95 to examine enemy wire & found it to be broken which forming a good outline. Relieved by 7th S.F. & moved back into reserve in GOMMECOURT with HQ at K.16.c.6.6.3.	
16th	2 Battalion on working party.	
17th	Relieved by 5th Lincs.	
18th	SOUASTRE	
19th	Marched to ST AMAND.	
	In billets.	

Army Form C. 2118.

WAR DIARY (4)
INTELLIGENCE SUMMARY.
(Erase heading not required.)

Instructions regarding War Diaries and Intelligence Summaries are contained in F. S. Regs., Part II. and the Staff Manual respectively. Title pages will be prepared in manuscript.

March 1917.

Hour, Date, Place	Summary of Events and Information	Remarks and References to Appendices
March 20th 1917	Marched to Poisson Farm.	Map:- AMIENS - 17 - 1/100,000 HAZEBROUCK 5A 1/100,000
21st "	" COURCELLES-au-BOIS.	
22nd "	Battalion engaged on Road Construction work about K.34.6, 95.10.	STRENGTH
23rd "	Marched to HARPONVILLE.	
24th "	COZY.	Off'rs O.R.
25th "	Review in form at BAOUEN & marched thence – 2 Coys to BAOUEN, remainder of Battalion to CRESUS.	Total 32. 906.
26th "	} Working on belts to SERVANS.	In trenches 22. 725.
27th "		
28th "	Entrained at BAOUEN at 10.0 p.m.	
29th "	Detrained at CHOCQUES about 6.0 p.m. marched to billets at RELY.	
30th "	In billets at RELY.	
31st "	" " " Gunning.	

R.H. Checkland Lieut. Col.,
Chg. 1/5" The Renwood Foresters –

To Headquarters,

      139th Infantry Brigade.

                            Herewith War Diary of my
Battalion for the month ending 30th April/17.

John P Raymond
Lieut & Adjutant
for Major,
cdg. 5th The Sherwood Foresters.

4/5/17-

WAR DIARY or INTELLIGENCE SUMMARY

Army Form C. 2118.

1/5 Notts & Derby R.

Hour, Date, Place	Summary of Events and Information	Remarks and References to Appendices
RELY — April 1st to April 12th	In G.H.Q. Reserve — Training	Map Ref: HAZEBROUCK 5A 1:100,000
13th	Marched to VENDIN-LEZ-BETHUNE	" 36C LENS SW 1:10000
14th	" NOEUX-LES-MINES — Transferred from III Corps to I Corps	Strengths: Offrs O.R — date Total strength 33. 890 } 5/4/17 For trenches 21. 604 }
15th	Marched to LES BREBIS	Total strength 31.866 For trenches 22.548 x
16th to 19th	Battalion employed on Road Construction Work.	x two platoons in rotation, not available for trenches
20th	Division relieved 24th Division on Right of Corps Front – Battalion moved to MARQUEFFLES FARM	Casualties Killed 2 Other Ranks Missing 1 Offr & 3 O.R. Wounded 1 " 11 "
21st & 22nd	at MARQUEFFLES FARM.	6 " (at duty) Evac. Div Area 48 "
23rd	At 4.45 a.m 6th & 8th Battalions attacked HILL 65 and FOSSE 3. Battalion relieved 6th Sherwood Foresters on Right of Brigade Front. 2 Companies on Outpost line with posts at M.30.a.9.4; M.30.a.5.7; M.30.a.8.3; M.30.a.9.7; M.30.a.8.8; M.24.c.9.0; M.24.c.8.2; M.24.c.9.3; M.24.c.6.3; 1 Company in Support — 1 Platoon at M.29.d.7.8 with	Reinforcements 2 Offrs & 21 Other Ranks

Army Form C. 2118.

WAR DIARY
or
INTELLIGENCE SUMMARY.
(Erase heading not required.)

Instructions regarding War Diaries and Intelligence Summaries are contained in F. S. Regs., Part II. and the Staff Manual respectively. Title pages will be prepared in manuscript.

Hour, Date, Place	Summary of Events and Information	Remarks and References to Appendices
April 23rd	fronts M.29.b.8.8. and M.23.d.9.2; One platoon M.30.a.05 north front M.30.a.06; One Platoon M.29.b.6. One Company in Reserve about M.28.d.9.2. Battalion H.Q - M.28.b.35.15. - 7th Battn. Sherwood Foresters on left; 95th Infantry Brigade on right. Enemy very active with trench mortars, machine guns and Rifle Grenades. Communication with front line Companies difficult except by night.	
24th	Battalion front extended as far N. as M.24.c.10.35. Battalion H.Q. were shelled about 11.0am with 5.9"- a stack of German Gas shells being exploded. Patrol reached Battalion of 10th Canadian Infantry Brigade now on Right during the night.	
25th	Patrol from 50th Canadians reported to Right Company that they had a listening post at M.30.c.8.1. Enemy artillery very active.	

WAR DIARY or INTELLIGENCE SUMMARY.

Army Form C. 2118.

Hour, Date, Place	Summary of Events and Information	Remarks and References to Appendices
April 26.	Work commenced on Defence Line – 8 fire trenches dug approx. on line M.29.b.62 – M.29.b.87 – M.23.d.91 – Enemy very active with Artillery, Trench Mortars and Machine Guns. "STOKES" Mortars fired 63 rounds on houses at M.30.b.00.35. Enemy endeavoured to strengthen his wire during the night; his working parties were dispersed by Lewis Gun & Rifle Grenade fire.	
27	Enemy holding his trenches very strongly – one man about every two yards. During the day numbers of the enemy seen at different points – Our snipers availed themselves of all targets. In retaliation for our artillery fire, enemy carried out an intense bombardment on our front from about 5.35 a.m – 6.15 a.m. A number of the houses on the Outpost line were demolished by Heavy Trench Mortars & in some cases the posts were partially buried. During the bombardment the enemy was seen to 'man' his firestep along the whole front – 6 and men got on to the parapet at intervals – 2 of these were shot. Between 10.0 and 11.0 p.m an enemy working party at M.30.b.27 was dispersed by Lewis Gun fire & Rifle Grenades. Work continued during the night on the defence line. Reserve Company (H) relieved the Support Company (E).	
28.	Captain Stone took out a patrol to ascertain condition of enemy wire in front of M.24.d.25.20 – M.24.d.40.30	

WAR DIARY or INTELLIGENCE SUMMARY

Army Form C. 2118.

Hour, Date, Place	Summary of Events and Information	Remarks and References to Appendices
28th	Artillery duel from 4.30am - 5.30am. Trench mortars, machine guns, snipers gave considerable trouble. Work on Defence line continued. Enemy fired between 40 or 50 gas shells on left Company front. Captain A. Stone, 2nd Lieut Jones & 2nd Lieut H.P.H. Martin and 50 Other Ranks of "C" Coy attempted to raid enemy trenches and house about M.24.d.30.25. They were discovered on the enemy front and bombs were compelled to withdraw. We suffered the following casualties: Captain Stone (missing), 2nd Lieut Jones, severely wounded; 3 Other Ranks missing; 7 Other Ranks wounded. Patrols went out immediately, & party had withdrawn to search for Captain Stone & the other missing men but met with no success. Our artillery barrage was very effective, and succeeded in knocking out an enemy machine gun firing from a house on Hill 65. They also silenced a machine-gun which was enfilading ABSALOM Trench from M.24.d.95.40. Two front line Companies co-operated with Rifle & Lewis gun fire & Rifle Grenades - Machine Gun Company also opened fire & Reserve Gun was out.	

WAR DIARY
or
INTELLIGENCE SUMMARY.

(Erase heading not required.)

Army Form C. 2118.

Instructions regarding War Diaries and Intelligence Summaries are contained in F. S. Regs., Part II. and the Staff Manual respectively. Title pages will be prepared in manuscript.

Hour, Date, Place	Summary of Events and Information	Remarks and References to Appendices
April 29th	Usual enemy activity - further work on defence line carried out. Fighting patrol sent out to search for our "missing Officer" men, also in the hope that a German patrol may be encountered, but without result. Patrol was sent to 10 attalion on right during the night	
30th	At 4.30 am gas was projected from BOIS-DE-RIAUMONT on to HILL 65 and train A redoubts of FOSSE 3. Heavy hostile artillery fire from 4.30 am to 5.0 am. Enemy still holding his trenches in force. Battalion relieved by 6th NORTH STAFFS during night and moved back to billets in BULLY GRENAY. Several cases of cerebro Spinal Meningitis occurred during the month	

John R. Hurt?
Lieut & Adjutant
for Major
Cdg. 1/5th The Sherwood Foresters

To Headquarters
139th Infantry Brigade

Herewith War
Diary for Month ending 31st
May, 1917.

G.C.Gilligan.
                    Major
cdg 1/5 The Sherwood Foresters.

3/6/17.

Army Form C. 2118.

WAR DIARY
OF
INTELLIGENCE SUMMARY.
(Erase heading not required.)

1/5th The Seaforth Highlanders

MAY - 1917 -

Instructions regarding War Diaries and Intelligence Summaries are contained in F.S. Regs., Part II. and the Staff Manual respectively. Title pages will be prepared in manuscript.

Hour, Date, Place	Summary of Events and Information	Remarks and references to Appendices
BULLY GRENAY. May 1st 1917	In Divisional Reserve in Billets at BULLY GRENAY.	Ref. Capt LEWIS. 36 C.S.W./1000
6th	2nd in Comd - Lt. Col. D.H. CHECKLAND D.M.C. ceased to command the Battalion.	Strength 3.5.17. Off. 28 Batt'n 873 Base. 18
6th & 7th	Relieved 4th Lincolnshire Regt. in Brigade Support PIERRE road section in vicinity of M10 & M4. Digging and work carried on in support of M10 a & M4. During the day. Major C.C. CURRIE M.C. A.I.S. assumed command of Battn. 10 inst.	Reinforcing draft. 2 Officers - 42 O.R.
12th	Relieved 6th Seaforth Borderers in Right Subsector - 7.2.13 an Off. and 138th Brigade on right.	Casualties: Killed Off. - Wounded - Off. 2 " (slightly) " 1 (acc.) 1
13th / 18th	In Trenches - Line held by 2 Coys with 2 Coys in. M12 C. MOS along Q.M.S.H. CZAR and COOPER TRENCHES to N.C. During this time work was concentrated on improvement of defences. Enemy. Very active with artillery + Trench Mortars.	ORs 46 " 5 " 3
19th	Relieved by 6th N Staff.- Moved back into Divisional Reserve at BULLY GRENAY.	Evacuated sick unser S. 2219. Off. - " 4
20th / 24th	In Divisional Reserve at BULLY GRENAY.	Off. - OR 16
25th	Relieved 4th Lincolnshire Regiment in Brigade Reserve LIEVIN Sect'r - Billets in Cellars. HQ REDMAS (19.7.2.7.8) in vicinity. Battn at work nightly improving defences of Lieven.	Strength 31/5/17. Off. 32 Batt'n 809 Base. 211 Reinf. 293
26th / 30th	In Brigade Reserve.	
31st	Relieved 6th C.S.W. Right Subsector. 10th Canadian Bgde took over on Right. 7th Border S.F. on left.	

G.C. Gilligan Major

Cmd'g 1/5th The Seaforth Highlanders

WAR DIARY
INTELLIGENCE SUMMARY.
1/5th The Sherwood Foresters

Army Form C. 2118.

Vol 26

H.26

June 1917 —

Hour, Date, Place	Summary of Events and Information	Remarks and references to Appendices

LIEVIN
June 1st 1917
	In trenches LIEVIN Sector - SOUCHEZ RIVER - M.24.a.95.23. 10th Canadian Infantry Brigade on the right. 1/7th Sherwood Foresters left. Battalion H.Q. M.28.d.32.13.	Ref. map LENS - 36 c S.W. 1/10000
		Strength 1-6-17
		    O.R.
		Battn. Off. 813
		         32
		Trenches 24 493

" 2nd	At midnight Canadians on right unsuccessfully attacked the enemy positions on the right.	Casualties O.R. Killed - 4 Wounded 1 55 Missing - 2 Wounded at duty - 13
" 3rd 4th	11th Canadian Infantry Brigade relieved 10th Canadian Infantry Brigade on right.	Evacuated Divisional Area.
" 5th	Post established at M.24.c.94.05. 1/7th Batt. S.F. took over line from left company N. of M.24.c.63.55. At 3.30 a.m. Canadian troops on right occupied generating-station	O.R. 33
" 6th	Battalion relieved on front SOUCHEZ RIVER - M.30.a.88.62 - M.24.c.63.55 by 4th 5th Leicesters, and moved back into Divisional Reserve in BULLY GRENAY. During this time front was observed in consequence of which very active patrolling was carried out, and most useful information brought in.	Strength 28/6/17 Off. O.R. Battn. 31 721 Trenches 19 409
7th to 14th	At BULLY GRENAY Battalion engaged in working parties and training.	

WAR DIARY
INTELLIGENCE SUMMARY.
(Erase heading not required.)

Army Form C. 2118.

Hour, Date, Place	Summary of Events and Information	Remarks and references to Appendices
June 12th – 1917.	5th Lincolns successfully raided the enemy trenches at 1.0 a.m.	
15th	Relieved 5th North Staffs in Right Sub Sector, PIERRE Sector. 138th Infantry Brigade on right, 1st Sherwood Foresters on left. Batt. H.Q. M.11.d.55.45	
16th	In trenches.	
17th	In trenches.	
18th	2nd Durham L.I. 151st Inf. Bde., relieved 1st Sherwood Foresters on left.	
19th	At 3.0 a.m. gas successfully projected on areas N.19.a, N.13.a.r.c., N.1.f. At 3.0 p.m. 5th Leicesters attacked, captured & consolidated enemy trench system M.30.d.2.8 to M.30.f.15.50. – 3 Counter-attacks repulsed. Relieved by 1st Batt. S.F. "A" & "B" Companies under Captain Harking, M.C., moved back to billets in BULLY GRENAY & training for raid. Remainder of Battalion moved to CITÉ ST PIERRE. Battalion H.Q., M.16.d.55.93. During this time 1st Cavalry Division dug new front and support lines.	

Army Form C. 2118.

WAR DIARY
or
INTELLIGENCE SUMMARY.
(Erase heading not required.) (III)

Instructions regarding War Diaries and Intelligence Summaries are contained in F. S. Regs., Part II. and the Staff Manual respectively. Title pages will be prepared in manuscript.

Hour, Date, Place	Summary of Events and Information	Remarks and references to Appendices
June 20th 1917	In support - 2 Companies training. Remainder of	
21st	Battalion engaged in working parties.	
22nd		
23rd	Relieved 6th Batt. L.F. in Left Sub-Sector - PIERRE Sector.	
	1st Norwood Trenches on Right, 18th Inf. Bde on Left.	
24th	At 9.30 p.m, 139th Brigade on right captured and consolidated	
	AHEAD and ADMIRAL Trenches.	
25th	At 12-45 am the enemy line was successfully raided between	
	points N.1.d.16.44 and N.1.d.11.20 by 'A' & 'B' Companies.	
	Strength 6 Officers and 110 Other Ranks. Gaps in enemy	
	wire, through which parties entered enemy trenches had	
	been very satisfactorily cut by 19th Siege Battery. All	
	parties reached their objectives and remained in	
	enemy line 30 minutes. A number of dead were found	
	in enemy line, presumably killed by Artillery	
	Barrage. The remainder of the enemy put up some	
	show of resistance & were either bayoneted & bombed.	
	Total of 10 killed & 1 wounded by raiding party is estimated.	
	At 21 killed & a considerable number wounded. A number of	

WAR DIARY
or
INTELLIGENCE SUMMARY.

(Erase heading not required.) IV

Army Form C. 2118.

Hour, Date, Place	Summary of Events and Information	Remarks and references to Appendices
June 25th/17	The enemy were heard in dug-outs which were heavily bombed. A party of about 5 of the enemy surrendered to an officer man & passed back to be sent over to our lines. One only of these was brought in & he died about 1 hour afterwards. The remainder appear to have offered resistance & further details as to this party is obscure. Our casualties were eight. Killed ... 2 Missing ... 2 Wounded ... 9	
26th	Both the "missing" are known to have got clear of enemy lines. A patrol searched for these men until daylight. Right of Division & Corps sought advanced with little opposition in consequence of which active patrolling was carried out to ascertain if enemy were holding trenches on our front normally & this was found to be so.	
27th "	Corps on right occupied LA COULOTTE. Strong patrols on our front found enemy holding his line of opposing trenches as usual. Relieved by 6th Batt. S.F. & moved back into Support in CITE-ST- PIERRE. Batln. H.Q. M.19. d.55.93	

WAR DIARY
or
INTELLIGENCE SUMMARY. V
(Erase heading not required.)

Army Form C. 2118.

Hour, Date, Place	Summary of Events and Information	Remarks and references to Appendices
June 28/1917.	At 7.10 p.m. 138th and 139th Infantry Brigades operations revealed enemy trenches on our right. At the same time the Canadian Corps on right of the Division & the 6th Division on the left co-operated. This Battalion carried out a feint attack with dummies in connection with above operations on the line M.18.d.60.52 – N.1.c.40.30. This was completely successful.	
29th "	Ten Junkers.	
30th "	At 2-34 a.m. the 7th Batt. threw out patrols on its right which reconnoitred enemy line in our Right Battalion front. At 11-0 p.m. Battalion commenced to move forward for attack on enemy line on front N.13.a.90.65 to N.13.d.15.70	

G.G. Gilligan, Lieut. Colonel.
Cdg. 1/5th Sherwood Foresters.

WAR DIARY

INTELLIGENCE SUMMARY

1/5th Bn. The Sherwood Foresters
(Notts and Derby Regt. T.F.)

Army Form C. 2118.

13/46

H.27

Hour, Date, Place	Summary of Events and Information	Remarks and References to Appendices
CITE ST. THEODORE July 1st 1917	At 2.47am the Battalion with 3 Coys in line & one in support reached the enemy frontline east of ASN, landing on the objective N13d 10.65 - N13a 98.65 in co-operation with 2nd Bn N.F. on right and 6th Bn N[?] on left. Left Company reached objective by 4.15am and Centre Company by 5.00am. Right Company failed to reach their objective. Rifle and MG fire was encountered. Enemy shots were small parties over the open as soon as it became light, all of which were repulsed with heavy loss to own loss. Own guns opened fire. This big support the enemy launched a strong counter attack at about 6.30am by bombing along trench at N13a 95.65. This advance was all repulsed. One of bombing our advance over the open from the south in the neighbourhood of COTTON TRENCH. The counter attack across the open was all repulsed with loss. At the end of the night some attempt was made by our own bombers who threw enough into our line at about N13a 95.65 and N13a 02.15. The enemy party came quickly there our own in No Mans Land. He fired waves of which are accounted for to a man by our Lewis Gun fire. He too suffered severe [loss] by our enemy garrison in addition a number of our officers & mountain of his [?] and 3 other [?] and the [?] had many prisoners of being out off ultimately by [?] by covering No Mans Land. Out of [?] & were to be [?]	Map 36c SW1 (trenches) Map 36.3 (trenches) Map 36c N.W.3 (trenches) Casualties 2-6-17 Off O.R. Killed — 33 Brn'd — 74 Gassed 1 119 Reinforcements received Month = 2 Off. 245 O.R. Lieut. Emanuelli joined R'on = 28 O.R.

2.

Instructions regarding War Diaries and Intelligence Summaries are contained in F. S. Regs., Part II. and the Staff Manual respectively. Title pages will be prepared in manuscript.

WAR DIARY

~~or~~

~~INTELLIGENCE~~ SUMMARY. 1/5th Bn The Sherwood Foresters (Notts and Derby Regt) T.F.

(*Erase heading not required.*)

Army Form C. 2118.

Hour, Date, Place	Summary of Events and Information	Remarks and References to Appendices
July 1st, 1917 (contd)	been the principal cause of the retirement. The 2 officers of the Support Company with about 40 men established and held a position in ALARM trench and finally consolidated at the Railway about N.13.c.72.20 where they repulsed a counter attack later in the day. This position was handed over to the 8th Sherwood For. 139th Inf. Bde. on relief. The mixture of units, the fact that at least one Coy of the Batn on the right (2nd Bn S.S.) had missed direction, and the fact that both officers of our right Coy became casualties before reaching the enemy front line, prevented that portion of the attack from reaching their objective. The enemy appear to have counter attacked both over the open and down trenches and reached the German front line at about N.13.c.65.70, and in the railway cutting to the North. It was from this direction that the counter attack on the Right of my Centre Company developed. The lack of time for preparation and reconnaissance, the length of my front and the depth of the objective, having regard to the number of men at my disposal, the darkness of the night which rendered it very easy for direction to be lost, were all factors which seemed to make the chances of a successful attack negligible, if, as proved to be the case, the enemy had any real intention of holding this portion of the line.	Total Casualties during Month:- Officers: Missing - 4 Wounded - 1 Other Ranks:- Killed - 14 Missing - 62 Wounded - 78 Wdd (at duty) - 3

Army Form C. 2118.

WAR DIARY
INTELLIGENCE SUMMARY.

1/5th Bn. The Sherwood Foresters (Notts-Derby Regt) T.F

(Erase heading not required.)

Hour, Date, Place	Summary of Events and Information	Remarks and References to Appendices
July 1st 1917 (Cont.)	Remnants of Battalion who were up to make the attack, 8 officers 270 O.R. Lost casualties during the Operation Officers & Men 1 Dead, 1 Pris. injured. Other ranks Killed 13, Missing 62, Wounded 81.	
2nd 1917.	During the early hours the Battalion was relieved by 8/2 Sherwood Foresters and 9/ Norfolk, 71st Inf. Bde. A Composite Company was formed from the remnants of the Battalion and on relief moved into support of the 6th Sherwood Foresters in the Reserve trenches of the CITE ST PIERRE SECTOR. Remnants of the Battalion including Bn. HQ moved into Brigade Support for the CITE ST PIERRE Sector.	
3rd 1917.	Relieved by 2/6 (Hackney) Battalion Canadian Infantry and moved back to BULLY GRENAY.	
4th 1917	3.0 am Entrained at BULLY GRENAY for MAGNICOURT COMTÉ.	
5th 1917 to 22nd 1917	Battalion re-organising and training at MAGNICOURT.	
23rd 1917	Marched to VERQUIN.	
24th "	Marched to LABOURSE.	
25 " "	Marched to PHILOSOPHE. Relieved Brigade Support for CITE ST ELIE Sector CITE ST. ELIE Left). 2 Companies in Support to Bogue Basin (6" Bn S.F.).	
26th 1917 to 29th 1917	In Both Support. Battalion engaged nightly on Working Parties.	

Army Form C. 2118.

WAR DIARY
INTELLIGENCE SUMMARY.
1/5 Bn. The Sherwood Foresters
(Notts and Derby Regt) T/-

(Erase heading not required.)

Instructions regarding War Diaries and Intelligence Summaries are contained in F. S. Regs., Part II. and the Staff Manual respectively. Title pages will be prepared in manuscript.

Hour, Date, Place	Summary of Events and Information	Remarks and References to Appendices
July 30th 1917	Relieved 6th Bn. Sherwood Foresters in Right Subsector G.T.S F.W.K Sector G.12.a.75.10 (WERMBURG-HARWICH Road) - G.12.c.20.85. 13th Bgde. Bde on Right. 7th Sherwood Brelow on Left. Battalion H.Q. G.H.A.52.15. Lane Farm. by posts. 3 Companies in the line, 1 in Support. Relieved with 2 Companies of 6th Bn. S.F. Trenches in a very bad condition owing to wet weather. Rations & stores brought up to Battn. H.Q. by tramway. Considerable enemy aerial operations. Carrying parties between Caves & Elsie & Quarrie frequently seen but no opportunities of the enemy offered. Our Aircraft favourable. In front.	Strength Off O.R. Relief 23 740 Trench 15 387
31st 1917	In trenches.	

B.W. Vann Major.
Cmg 1/5th Bn. The Sherwood Foresters.

WAR DIARY
INTELLIGENCE SUMMARY.
(Erase heading not required.)

1/5 Nott & Derby
13/46 August 1917

Hour, Date, Place	Summary of Events and Information	Remarks and references to Appendices
Cts.F.E.F.		Reference Maps LOOS 36cNW3 LA BASSEE 36cNW1 (1/5000) & BETHUNE (outline) 1/20000
August 1st/1917. 6ᵃ / 4ᵃ	In trenches. Right sector Cts.F.E.F. K. C.T.O.R	Strength Off 15 Total 26 O.R 387 738
5ᵃ	Relieved by 6" S² & moved back into Bayart Support at PH10.10.30.45. 300 Enemy shells fell m.b. PH10.10.30.45	
6ᵃ 6ᵃ 9ᵃ	In Bayart Reserve. 2 Companies preparing for practising raid on Enemy trench.	Reinforcements 10 Off. 41 Other Ranks.
10:55	Relieved 6" Sherwood Foresters in trenches - immediately after taking over 9" Coy captains one prisoner outside own wire	
11ᵃᵃ 6ᵃ 12ᵃ	In trenches.	Evacuated Insconence & Sick 16 O.R.
13:55	2 Companies of 6" S² Sherwood Foresters raided the enemy trenches from our front at 10:30pm.	
14?	At 2 and B & D Companies raided the enemy trenches between the following points. Enemy front line:- H.13.a.16.95 to G.12.a.98.86 " Support " :- H.7.c.38.00 to H.7.c.10.40 (Continued)	

WAR DIARY
INTELLIGENCE SUMMARY
(Erase heading not required.)

Army Form C. 2118.

August 1917.

Hour, Date, Place	Summary of Events and Information	Remarks and references to Appendices
August 14th/17 (Cont'd)	Three attempts excepted in the capture of 2 prisoners of the 128th Reserve Regiment. Casualties were inflicted on the enemy & several dugouts destroyed. Our casualties were — Killed 1, Wounded 11, Missing 3.	Casualties: Killed - 1 Officer, 4 O.R.s. Wounded - 20 ", " (at duty) 3 ", Missing - 3 ".
15th	Canadian Corps (on Right) successful in attacks at N. of LENS.	
16th	Relieved by 5th LINCOLNS. Marched back to VEROUIN in Divisional Reserve.	
17th	At VEROUIN. Bn. inspected by G.O.C. Division.	
18th	At VEROUIN.	
19th	Marched to FOUQUIERES by BETHUNE.	
20th	Battalion training at FOUQUIERES.	
21st		
22nd		
23rd		
24th	46th Division relieved the Brigade in front Northwards taking over the front of one Brigade of 2nd Division. 139th Inf. Bde. relieving 99th Inf. Bde on the CAMBRIN Sector. Battalion moved into Brigade Support & relieved 1st ROYAL BERKS. Battalion H.Q. & 2 Companies at ANNEQUIN, 2 Companies	

(3)

WAR DIARY

INTELLIGENCE SUMMARY.

Army Form C. 2118.

August 1917.

Hour, Date, Place	Summary of Events and Information	Remarks and references to Appendices
August 26/7 (cont)	in immediate Support to Right Batt'n (6th Sherwood Foresters), 1 Coy in Support & ½ Coy in immediate Support to Left Batt'n (8th Sherwood Foresters).	Strength 30/8/17 O.B. Offs 22 440 Other Ranks 34 721
27/8 28/8 29/8	In Brigade Support.	

C.G. Giligan, Lieut. Col.,
Cmdg 1/5 Bn. The Sherwood Foresters.

WAR DIARY
of
INTELLIGENCE SUMMARY.
(Erase heading not required.)

Army Form C. 2118.

September 1917. 1/5 N. Yorks, Dewby

Hour, Date, Place	Summary of Events and Information	Remarks and references to Appendices

ANNEQUIN.

Sept 1st 1917 — Batt relieved 6th Berwick Fusiliers in CAMBRIN Right Subsector.

2nd — "

3rd — At 4:30am quite a heavy bombardment on enemy part of about 170 being attempted to enter our trenches. The raid was repulsed, 1 prisoner being left on our wire.

4th — " in trenches

5th — "

6th — Batt relieved by 6th Cheshire Bn and moved back into Divisional Reserve at BEUVRY & BETHUNE.

7th — At Div Reserve training.

8th — "
9th — "
10th — "
11th — "
12th — Batt relieve 6th R.F. in CAMBRIN Right Subsector.

13th — In trenches — Enemy very quiet during this tour.

14th —
15th —
16th —
17th —
18th —
19th — Batt relieved by 1st Bn the Royal Scots 99th Infy Bde. 2nd Division &
20th — moved back to SAILLY LABOURSE. Transport & HQrs moved to VERQUIGNEUL.

21st — At SAILLY LABOURSE. 139th Inf Bde H.Q. 46th Division relieved 7.25 and 18th Inf Bde. 6th Division Battalion in Reserve H.26 c.7.70.

Relieved by LABOURSE from 1003 Hours
36.8. Hours

Strength
Off. 32
Other Ranks 419. 364
Total 32 727. 391

Reinforcements
9 Off. 23 O.R.

Casualties
Killed — 1
Wounded — 2
Wounded at duty — 1 18
(not evac) 3

Evacuated sick cases
3 Off. 26 O.R.

H.29

Army Form C. 2118.

WAR DIARY
or
INTELLIGENCE SUMMARY.
(Erase heading not required.)

September 1917.

Hour, Date, Place	Summary of Events and Information	Remarks and references to Appendices
September 27th (cont'd) 22nd	and N. 2 & 5D.80, vis H.14.70 Secto. Other Battalions moving onto Brigade Supports. 2 Coys in O.B.1. 1 Coy on O.B.1 and 1 Coy on HINDU TRENCH, with Coy. H.Q. at H31.c.07.45, H31.a.90.55. H.31.a.60.80; x H.31.b.10.90. Batt. H.Q. G.30.d.8.2.	Strength
23rd to 27th	Sie Brigade Support. First lots of salvage work carried out. Carrying rations & rum for 6th Bn. S.L.	
28th	Bn. relieved 6th L.F. in Brigade Reserve. H.14. 70 Sects one front N.2.c.5.8.6. H.32.a.5.8.3.7. 7th Bn. H.P. H.3.d. 01.20. 7th Bn. S.R. on left. 10th Son. Aus. 6th Bde on right. 39th Somerset (Riveters) Division opposite.	March Relief
29th	In Reserve. 2 men from A Coy on duty as Lewis or Hunt Trench railway	
30th	In Reserve	Off OR 1 169/279 11 16 770 720

John M Raymond
Captain For Lieut Col.
Cdg 1/5 Bn. The Kings Own —

WAR DIARY
INTELLIGENCE SUMMARY
(Erase heading not required.)

Army Form C. 2118.

VII 30

October 1917

1/5th Bn. The Sherwood Foresters

Hour, Date, Place	Summary of Events and Information	Remarks and references to Appendices
HILL 70. Sect. LOOS. October 1st to 4th 1917.	In trenches – Hill 70. Right sect. Enemy quiet except on night of October 3rd when heavy bombardment preceded enemy raid on Battalions on our right and left. Colincamps – work on organising and improving trenches. In Brigade Reserve – MAZINGARBE – training.	Strength 4-10-17. O.R. Off. 26 474 T.O.R. 41 732
4th to 6th 1917		Reinforcements 5 Off. 630 O.R.
10th & 16th 1917	In trenches – Enemy not quiet. Nothing of moment occurred during tour. Wet weather caused trenches to be in very bad condition.	Casualties Off – O.R. Killed – 5 Wounded 1 12 Wounded – 1 (accident)
16th to 22nd 1917	In Brigade Support – Hard work for men on improving Communications and new trenches and carrying parties.	
23rd to 28th 1917	In trenches – Enemy remained quiet.	
28th to 31st 1917	In Brigade Reserve – MAZINGARBE – training.	Enc. Strength Area. 19 O.R. Strength 25.10.17 Off O.R. 22 443 Total 37 722

C.G.Gilligan
Lieut. Col.
Comg. 1/5th Bn The Sherwood Foresters

Army Form C. 2118.

WAR DIARY
of
INTELLIGENCE SUMMARY.

November 1917

1/5th Bn. Lincolnshire

(Erase heading not required.)

Instructions regarding War Diaries and Intelligence Summaries are contained in F.S. Regs., Part II. and the Staff Manual respectively. Title pages will be prepared in manuscript.

Hour, Date, Place	Summary of Events and Information	Remarks and references to Appendices
HULLUCH Sector LOOS		Strength 2-11-17.
November 1st & 3rd 1917	2 Brigade Reserve. MAINGARBE. training.	O.R.
3rd & 9th "	2 weeks. H.Q. to Right sector. Enemy quiet. work	Officers 29 436
9th & 14th "	Concentrated on wiring.	Joined 40 719
	2 Brigade support.	Reinforcements
NOYELLES		O.R. 2nd
November 14th & 15th "	2 Brigade Reserve. Battalion relieved by 4th Lincolnshire Regt.	Rejoined from hospital Oct. 1
N. ELIE Right Sector		Casualties
November 15th & 22nd "	2 Trenches. Battalion relieved 4th Lincolnshire Regiment	Officers O.R.
	Enemy very quiet except for trench mortar activity.	Wounded 1 15*
FOUQUIERES		* 2 wounded accidentally.
November 22nd & 29th "	Battalion relieved by 6th Bn. Sherwood Foresters. 2 Brigade	9 wounded remained at duty.
	Reserve. training.	Strength 3-11-17.
VERQUIN		Officers O.R.
November 27th & 28th "	2 Brigade Reserve. VERQUIN.	Strength 19 411
N. ELIE Right Sector		Joined 35 705
November 28th & 30th "	2 Trenches. Considerable artillery and trench mortar activity by	Evacuated sick and Area
	enemy.	M.E. O.R.
		6 21

G.G. Gilligan
Lt Col
C/O 15th Bn Lincolnshire

WAR DIARY

December 1917

Army Form C. 2118.

INTELLIGENCE SUMMARY

(Erase heading not required.) 1/5th Bn The Sherwood Foresters

Hour, Date, Place	Summary of Events and Information	Remarks and references to Appendices
ST. ELIE RIGHT SECTOR December 1st to 3rd.	In trenches – Enemy quiet with exception of trench mortar + artillery activity.	Reference map LOOS 36 C N W 3 1/10 000 Strength Off. O.R. French 70 411 Total 34 693
VERQUIN December 3rd to 9th.	Divisional Reserve – In training for raid on enemy trenches.	Reinforcements 6 Officers 8 + O Ranks.
ST ELIE RIGHT SECTOR December 9th to 15th	In trenches – Wiring + improving trenches. Artillery + trench mortar activity on both sides.	Evacuated Divisional Base - Sick 104 9 Other Ranks.
Dec. 11th 3·40 A.M.	The Battn successfully raided 3 lines of enemy trenches. Captured 5 prisoners and a light machine gun doing much damage on his trenches. Our casualties were Other Ranks:- 2 missing 2 killed 22 wounded	Casualties Officers O.Ranks Killed – 3 Wounded + returned off – 28 do remained at duty 4 Missing – 2
PHILOSOPHE Dec 15th to 21st	In Brigade Reserve. 1 Coy being in line in support to Left Bn right. " " " " " Left. Carrying + working parties being provided by each Coy. Companies in PHILOSOPHE change over with those companies in support + provide necessary carrying and working parties	
ST ELIE RIGHT SECTOR December 21st to 27th	In trenches – Wiring Artillery + trench mortar fairly active on both sides.	H·21

2.

WAR DIARY
or
INTELLIGENCE SUMMARY.
(Erase heading not required.) 1/5th Batt. The Sherwood Foresters

Army Form C. 2118.

December 1917

Hour, Date, Place	Summary of Events and Information	Remarks and references to Appendices
		Strength Off. O.Ranks
		Trench 73 432
		Total 38 730
VERQUIN December 2nd to 31.	In Divisional Reserve – Training.	
	C.G. Geigier	
	Lieut Colonel.	
	Comg 1/5th Bn Sherwood Foresters	

Army Form C. 2118.

WAR DIARY January 1918
OF
INTELLIGENCE SUMMARY.
(Erase heading not required.) 1/5th Bn The Loyal North Lancs

Instructions regarding War Diaries and Intelligence Summaries are contained in F. S. Regs., Part II. and the Staff Manual respectively. Title pages will be prepared in manuscript.

Hour, Date, Place	Summary of Events and Information	Remarks and References to Appendices
VERQUIN Jany 1st to Jany 3rd	In Divisional Reserve – Training.	Rifle Stgh 2000 36 O/R 3/10/00 **Strength** Off. OR Trench 79 440 Total 37 739
ST. ELIE RIGHT SECTOR. Jany 3rd to Jany 9th	In trenches – Heavy snow. Enemy quiet.	**Reinforcements** 15 Officers 233 O.Ranks
PHILOSOPHE Jany 9th to Jany 17th	In Brigade Reserve. Two Companies in the line in support to 6th and 8th Bn SHERWOOD FORESTERS. Anticipated relief by 11th DIVISION was postponed owing to condition of roads following rain and thaw after protracted frost.	Evacuated sick to Field Ambulance 1 Off. 17 O.R. **Casualties** Killed Nil Wounded 3 O.Ranks and 2 O.R. accidental duty
ST ELIE RIGHT SECTOR. Jany 17th to Jany 22nd	In Trenches. Enemy exceptionally quiet except to a Divisional Relief Trench Mortar towards Very wet. The Bn was relieved on the night of January 22nd by the 9th Bn LANCASHIRE FUSILIERS and billeted for the night at SAILLY LABOURSE.	

WAR DIARY
or
INTELLIGENCE SUMMARY.
(Erase heading not required.)

Army Form C. 2118.

Hour, Date, Place	Summary of Events and Information	Remarks and References to Appendices
LAPUGNOY Jany 28th to Jany 31st.	On Jany 28th Bn. marched from SAILLY LABOURSE to billets at LAPUGNOY. In Billets. Remaining on Jany 31st. The Bn. formed part of a Guard of Honour at the presentation of medal ribbons by I Army Commander, and was congratulated by the G.O.C. on their turn out and smartness. On January 28th the 1/7 th Bn. SHERWOOD FORESTERS was disbanded and this Bn was reinforced by a large draft of Officers and men from that Bn. O.C.Gillespie Lieut Col. Comdg 1/5th Bn Sherwood Foresters	Strength Offs O.Ranks Trench 34 546 Total 51 943

WAR DIARY February 1918

1/5 N'th & Derby

Army Form C. 2118.

INTELLIGENCE SUMMARY.
(Erase heading not required.)

Place	Hour, Date	Summary of Events and Information	Remarks and References to Appendices

LAPUGNOY	Feby 1st & 2nd
	" 3rd
	" 4th & 5th
	" 6th
	" 7th
		Route march - Musketry & Lewis Gun practice & bathing. Armoury and Lewis Gun Cleaners.
		Church Parade
		Musketry - Platoon & Company drill. Armoury & Lewis Gun Classes.
		Road March - Tactical Scheme for Officers
		Intercoy Economy
			Reference Maps
			HAZEBROUCK 5A 1/100,000
			Strength 1-2-18 Offrs OR
			        French 34 526
			        Total 57 943

AUCHY-AU-BOIS	Feby 8th	Batt marched to AUCHY-AU-BOIS en route to DOMY training area	
ERNY ST JULIEN	Feby 9th	Bn marched to ERNY ST JULIEN - Marching and GOC North Division at FEBVIN PALFART in connection with the move of the Division into a Divisional concentration scheme.	Reinforcements 1113 Other Ranks
	Feby 11th - 12th Feby 13th - 16th	Inter-company Rathos cleaning Musketry. Musketry - Platoon & Company Drill & Tactical formation & extended order Will. Criterion were recognised as a 4 platoon basin. Tactical exercises for Officers NCOs & heard Two platoons - Bombers & Lewis Gun Classes	Evacuated Divisional Area Sick 19 Other Ranks Rejoined Bn from Hospital 2 OR

	Feby 17th
	Feby 18th 20th
	Feby 21st
	Feby 22nd
		Church Parade addressed by B.G. Cmg the Brigade.
		Extended Order - Attack practice - Musketry - Classes - Mount & Lewis Gun practice.
		Interior Economy - Bathing - Musketry.
		Bathing on account attack scheme under Brigade Scheme. Lynd Col F.R. Harvey M.C. French
			Strength 16/2/18 Offrs OR
			                      34 592
			        Total 50 1078

	Feby 23rd Feby 24th - 26th Feby 27th	took over Command of the 2nd Bn & C.G. Guigan attended Commandant's Cert Reinforcement Camp. Inoculation. Artillery/mundan practice & special attack scheme.	
	Feby 28th	I Inst to Brigade Counter Attack scheme was carried out with the 6th Bn. The Newport Frontier under Divisional arrangements - No J. Reform B Company took the Brigade Platoon Competition under A.R.A rules Lieutenant Economy - Bathing - No 7 Platoon B Cy were deputed in the ARA Competition by Platoons from the 137th 138 139 Brigades	

Hansen Lieut Col
C/g 1/5th N. Regts Derby

Army Form C. 2118.

WAR DIARY / INTELLIGENCE SUMMARY.

1/5th Batt. The Loyal North Lancs.

March 1918

(Erase heading not required.)

Hour, Date, Place	Summary of Events and Information	Remarks and References to Appendices
ERNY ST JULIEN 1st & 2nd	Practising for Batln. Platoon Competition.	Strengths 1-3-18. Officers. Other Ranks.
3rd	Church Service.	Batln. Strength 30 104
4th	Practising for Batln. Inter Platoon Competition	French " 34 592
AUCHY-AU-BOIS 5th	Marched to AUCHY-AU-BOIS and billeted for the night.	Casualties. Killed in Action 14 Other Ranks
LA PREOL 6th 7th 8th 9th 10th 11th 12th 13th	Entrained at AUCHY-AU-BOIS detrained BEUVRY and marched to LA PREOL. Training. Intakuday took for finale of platoon competition. Jethrey at BEUVRY. Firing on the range. Outer to taking over the line cancelled. Forms on the range and proceeded having Bayonet fighting drill to 2.00 December having Commanding Officer (Lieut Col. J.B. Lawson M.C.) took over Command of 130th Infantry Brigade. Major R. Hackney M.C. took over Command of Battn.	Wounded. 1 Off. 24 Other Ranks Wounded remained on duty. 1 Off. 4 Other Ranks Gassed N.Y.D. 2 Other Ranks Shell Shock N.Y.D. 1 Off. 3 Other Ranks Evacuated Convenient Sick. 1 Off. 41 Other Ranks
CAMBRIN SECTOR 14th	Took over new Brigade sector, relieving one company of 1/4th Leicesters on the right and 2 companies of 6/4th North Staffs on the Left Town of 6 days - Enemy shelling heavy.	Reinforcements 29 Other Ranks
	Work consisted of improving trenches & wiring.	Strengths 29-3-18 Officers. Other Ranks
BEUVRY 20th	Moved into Brigade Support. Two Companies + Headquarters at BEUVRY - One Company Nurse La H - One Company Factory Dugouts	Batln. Strength 47 941 French " 33 856
21st	2rd of Batln. at BEUVRY Bathing and Physical Drill	

Army Form C. 2118.

WAR DIARY March 1918
INTELLIGENCE SUMMARY.
(Erase heading not required.)

Instructions regarding War Diaries and Intelligence Summaries are contained in F. S. Regs., Part II. and the Staff Manual respectively. Title pages will be prepared in manuscript.

Hour, Date, Place	Summary of Events and Information	Remarks and References to Appendices
BEUVRY 21st/22nd	Enemy raided Brigade front - Heavy Hostile Artillery barrage put down & several of the dugouts occupied by Company in Factory dugouts blown in. Casualties 5 killed 18 wounded	
22nd 23rd	Companies at BEUVRY on range and having Baths. "B" Company in Factory Dugouts relieved by "C" Company from BEUVRY.	
ANNEQUIN 24th	Relieved 6th Bn Sherwood Foresters in ANNEQUIN and took over defence of ANNEQUIN locality. Found working parties in Lieut Col N.B.F. Laurie's M.C. required Baths and took over Command	
25th		
CITÉ ST PIERRE 27th	Brigade relieved by 32nd Infantry Brigade. 11th Devons Baths moved to CITÉ ST PIERRE and relieved 85th Canadian Baths in Sector	
ST. EMILE SECTOR LEFT SECTOR 28th 29th 30th	Relieved 38th Canadian Bn in the Line. Enemy raided our trenches (see attached report) Enemy's trenches & wiring. Patrols sent out and endeavoured to enter enemy's line, but were unable to find gaps in the wire	
31st	Work continued on trenches & wiring. Patrols still unable to enter enemy line owing to Hostile Patrols Machine Guns &c.	John Rowan 3 Capt for Lt/Col Cmg/5th Sherwood Foresters

TIME TABLE.

11-26pm.	S.O.S. ST. EMILE.
	(received from "A" Company (Right Company) repeated all companies 11-27.30pm.
11-26½pm.	Sent to Artillary.
11-27pm.	Sent to Brigade. 11-28p Flank Battns
11-34pm.	S.O.S. SAE. Advanced Company "D".
11-35pm.	Shells dropping short.
11-35½pm.	Barrage Lifts.
11-37pm.	C.O. speaks to O.C. "D" Company.
11-41pm.	Shells dropping short.
11-41pm.	Protect Mason.
11-46pm.	C.O. speaks to O.C. "A" Company.
11/46½pm.	C.O. speaks to "D" Company.
11-48pm.	C.O. speaks to "D" Company.
11-49pm.	Cease fire.

Total 23 minutes bombardment.

CASUALTY REPORT.

Lieut. H.W.Guichard.	N.Y.D. (Shell Shock).
5 Other Ranks.	N.Y.D. (Shell Shock).
6 Other Ranks.	Killed.
8 Other Ranks.	Wounded.

Total 1 Officer 20 Other Ranks.

1/5th Battalion, The Sherwood Foresters.

Report on Enemy Raid during night 29th/30th March, on the 1/5th Bn. The Sherwood Foresters.

At 10-40pm the enemy commenced a slow trench mortar and Prieste Bomb bombardment along our front and support line, from NABOB Alley to about line of Railway running through the centre of SATURDAY Post.

About 11-15pm this bombardment concentrated on to the front and support lines between N.8.b.40.15. to COSY Trench.

At 11-25pm as this bombardment appeared to be intensifying, the Right Company fired the S.O.S. Rocket, and sent the message by wire to Battalion Headquarters. Our Artillary barrage came down promptly. Shortly afterwards, our post at N.8.b.57.56. saw 14 Germans advancing near our wire. Rifle and Lewis Gun fire were opened, and the enemy disappeared towards his own line. It is believed that they suffered casualties, but no trace of these could be found later by our patrols.

Our Post in COMMOTION SAP was also attacked, and one of our men was killed by a bomb. The Post, however, succeeded in driving the enemy away by rifle fire and bombs at close quarters. Unfortunately the enemy T.M. Barrage was exceedingly accurate, and the garrisons of two of our posts were buried; several men killed and wounded and our trench considerably damaged. Owing to these circumstances there were not sufficient men immediately available to follow the enemy as he withdrew.

Our men shewed a fine spirit, and thanks to their steadiness, the enemy failed to enter our trenches or obtain identification.

Our Artillary Barrage appeared to have the effect of breaking up the raiders, as the two parties which reached our wire appeared to be quite disorganised and were probably part of a large party.

This is the fourth time in 20 days that he has raided the same area, his lack of artillery was very noticeable and only two or three guns were firing during the whole raid.

At 11-49pm the Front Line Companies reported that the raid had been successfully repulsed and our barrage was stopped.

The Raided Area included NUN'S Alley and COMMOTION SAPS and the ground in between.

Time Table and Casualty List attached.

Lieut. Colonel.
Cdg. 1/5th Bn. The Sherwood Foresters.

30/3/18.

139th Brigade.
46th Division.

1/5th SHERWOOD FORESTERS

APRIL   1918.

WAR DIARY / INTELLIGENCE SUMMARY

Army Form C. 2118

April 1918 1/5 North'n Derby

Hour, Date, Place	Summary of Events and Information	Remarks and references to Appendices
ST EMILE SECTION Sub-sector 1st and 2nd CITE ST PIERRE Sub & Sub	For the trenches – Mining – Patrolling active. Hostile action on both sides. French " Relieved by 1/8th Sherwood Foresters and moved into Brigade Reserve. In reserve – Working parties – Cité St Pierre subject to enemy gas shells	Strength 5.4.18 O/R 443 Total Strength 35 67 Casualties Killed 8 O/R Wounded 1 Off " Gassed - O/R " Shellshock 1 Off 2 O/R
ST EMILE SECTION Right Sub-sector Subs V.K. G.W.	Relieved by the 164th Sherwood Foresters Few trenches – Patrols active on L.H. side. Patrolling most active. Enemy patrol were active and attempted to cut out one of our posts but did not succeed. No artillery or trench mortar fire. 55th Division – Enterprise HQ also killed one German officer whose body was brought in. Patrols were again firing from the Boche. Few trenches. Artillery in Sabotting and Artillery on both sides continued.	Evacuated Sick Parade 43 Reinforcements 64
9h 10.4.14 BULLY GRENAY 11h/11.4.14 VERGUIN 12h HOUCHIN 12.4.14	Relieved by 52nd Canadian Batln 2.30am Headquarters & A&B Coy entrained for VERGUIN 11.30am C&D Companies entrained for HOUCHIN	Strength 26.4.18 O/R 543 Total Strength 1/5 82 French 32 413
VERGUIN to HOUCHIN 13h 14h 15h	Bathing – Lectures & Tactical Exercises Headquarters & A&B Coy march to HOUCHIN Musketry musketry – Special Bren Gun Classes commenced Reconnaissance of SAILLY LA BOURSE and NOYELLES beyond.	

WAR DIARY April 1918
INTELLIGENCE SUMMARY

Army Form C. 2118.

Hour, Date, Place	Summary of Events and Information	Remarks and references to Appendices
HOUCHIN 16th 17th	Our range firing practice – Lewis Gun Classes continue	
18th	Company and Platoon tactical scheme. Horse & Mule lines Defence scheme – Lectures – Lewis Gun classes continue	
	Orders Received to form up & move – Moved to CAMBRIN 1.30pm in support to 2nd Infantry Brigade. 1st Division with one Company in Bn. in support.	
	1st Bn. Northants Regiment also garrisoned in CAMBRIN. Lieut. Col. AE FARGUS MC admitted to Hospital. Major A HICKING MC took over Command of Bath. Our sector – Working parties for Front Brigade	
CAMBRIN to 23rd		
BEUVRY 22nd		
ESSARS SECTION		
24th to 24th	Relieved by 1st Bn Gloster Regiment & moved into billets	
25th to 24th 28th	Relieved 1st Bn Royal Scots Fusiliers in Brigade Reserve	
	In billets – Moving, digging &	
	1.30pm Enemy shelled Battn. HQ. Adjutant wounded, moved at duty	
VAUDRICOURT 26th/29th	Relieved by 1st/4th London Regiment & marched to VAUDRICOURT	
29th	Divisional Reserve – Billets in BURBURE	
30th	Interior Economy – Cleaning up, Bathing and training.	

A.V. Hawkin Lieut Col
Cmg 1st Bn The Bedfords Regiment

WAR DIARY
INTELLIGENCE SUMMARY.
(Erase heading not required.)

Army Form C. 2118.

May 1918 1/5 North Staffs

F.36

Hour, Date, Place	Summary of Events and Information	Remarks and References to Appendices
VAUDRICOURT		Strengths 3.5.18
1st	In bivouac – training	Offrs. O.R.
2nd	"Stood to" from 4.0am to 5.30am – Relieved 1/5th South Staffs	Bn. Strength 44 911
	in Left Sub-sector GORRE Section	French 31 643
GORRE Section		
3rd	Left Sub-sector – fairly quiet	Casualties
4th	Heavy bombardment on left	Killed 1 Offr. 6 O. Ranks
5th	Left sub-sector – fairly quiet	Wounded 1 " 17 "
6th	Relieved by 6th Cheshire Regt. & moved into Brigade Reserve	2 O. Ranks (Shell Gas N.Y.D)
7th	In reserve – All companies working – wiring re-	
8th }	Relieved the 8th Cheshire Foresters in Right sub-sector – Essarts-les-Béthune	Evacuated Sick Area
9th }	Right sub-sector – fairly quiet	3 Officers
10th	Relieved by 1/5th Lincolns & moved to BRIDGEHEAD	81 Other Ranks
	locality LE QUESNOY & "Stood to" all night	
VERQUIN 11th	Moved into Divisional Reserve at VERQUIN – Bathing	Reinforcements
12th	} Divisional Reserve } Standing to to move at one hour's	1 Officer
13th	} Intensive Training } notice during day and a moment's notice	82 Other Ranks
14th	} } at night	
ESSARS Section		
14th	Relieved 1/6th Bn. South Staffs Regt. in the Left Sub sector	
15th }	Shelling on both sides fairly active. Mining to	
16th }		
16th	Relieved by the 1/6th Bn. Cheshire Regt. Returned into	
	Brigade Reserve	

Army Form C. 2118.

WAR DIARY May 1918
INTELLIGENCE SUMMARY.
(Erase heading not required.)

Instructions regarding War Diaries and Intelligence Summaries are contained in F. S. Regs., Part II. and the Staff Manual respectively. Title pages will be prepared in manuscript.

Hour, Date, Place	Summary of Events and Information	Remarks and References to Appendices
ESSARS Section		Strength 3/5/18
17th	Brigade Relief - Bigg my line of resistance in Right sector	Total Strength 44 Offs. 892
18th	Relieved 158th Sherwood Foresters	Total Strength 19 479
19th	Enemy raided Right Coy front 18th & 19th defended each time without casualties to us. A number of rifle bombs	
20th	were afterwards found. Enemy gun shelling abnormal	
21st	during tour.	Lieut Col P.E.T. Tarvene M.C. Proceeded on leave 21/5/18.
22nd	Relief Completed - 138th Brigade which should have relieved	Major A. Hacking M.C. took over Command of Battn from that date.
	139th Brigade where 137th Brigade in GORRE	
	Sector owing to the large number of casualties caused	
	by gas shelling	
23rd	Right instructed Artillery active on both sides	
24th		
25th	Relieved by the 6th South Staffs and moved into Divisional	
26th	Reserve in Bivouacs VAUDRICOURT WOOD	
VAUDRICOURT		
26th	Interior Economy	
27th	Lectures to all Officers N.C.Os & all Companies by Div Gas Offr	
28th	Physical Training & Drill - Inspection by G.O.C. Division at Gosnay	Armstrong Major
	Ceremonial Parade	Cmdg 1/5th Sherwood Foresters
	Brigade	
	Afternoon bathing	
29th	Physical Training & Drill - Gosnay Ceremonial	
30th	Relieved 15th Leicester Regt in Brigade Reserve	
GORRE SECTION		
31st	West LOISNE Sentry & strengthening Cy positions. Artillery active.	

Mr Thomas

Army Form C. 2118.

WAR DIARY
or
INTELLIGENCE SUMMARY.
(Erase heading not required.)

June 1918   1/5 Notts & Derby   Vol 38

Instructions regarding War Diaries and Intelligence Summaries are contained in F. S. Regs., Part II. and the Staff Manual respectively. Title pages will be prepared in manuscript.

Place	Date	Hour	Summary of Events and Information	Remarks and references to Appendices
GORRE	1		In Brigade Reserve – Firing LOISNE Locality. Artillery active	
	2			
	3		Relieved 1/8th Sherwood Foresters in Right Sub-sector	4th June Lieut Col. M.P.X.X Pearson DSO.MC resigned comd. Leave to Eng. over command
	4			
	5			
	6		Fairly quiet tour	
	7			
VAUDRICOURT WOOD	8		Relieved by 1/6th North Staffs.	
	9		In Divisional Reserve	
	10		Interior Economy. Cleaning up &c for Ceremonial Parade – Bathing	
	11		2nd & 3rd Class ditto on range – Church Parade. Ceremonial Parade – Brigade formed Guard of Honour for presentation of Birthday Honours by Army Commander – (GOSNAY Chateau)	Lieut Col M.P.X. Taverner MS. Commanding Officer Lieut Col S.G. Gallagher late Command- ing Officer decorated D.S.O.
ESSARS Sector	11 to 17		Training and Interior Economy – Demonstration of Norwegian Company Rockets.	
	12 to 17			
	18/19		Relieved 1/5th Leicesters. Artillery active – great quantity of salvage including 18 pounder shells & quantity of agricultural implements. Successful raid on enemy line near LE TOURET (see note attached)	

H.37

Army Form C. 2118.

WAR DIARY June 1918.
INTELLIGENCE SUMMARY.
(Erase heading not required.)

Instructions regarding War Diaries and Intelligence Summaries are contained in F. S. Regs., Part II. and the Staff Manual respectively. Title pages will be prepared in manuscript.

Place	Date	Hour	Summary of Events and Information	Remarks and references to Appendices
ESSARS Section				Strength 16/18 Offrs OR
	19/20		Relieved by 1/6th N. Staffs.	Bn Strength 44 892
VERQUIN				Trench " 19 479
VAUDRICOURT WOOD			H.Q. Details & 'A' + 'B' Companies } In Divisional Reserve	Casualties -
			'C' + 'D' Companies	Killed 1 Off. 3 O.R.
	20		Interior Economy & Cleaning up	Wounded 2 " 36 "
	21		Practicing with No 36 grenades. Inspection of Arms by Armourer Sgt. Bathing	Mil: duty 6 "
	22		Reorganization of Platoons - Drill.	Evacuated -
	23		Divine Service.	3 Officers
GORRE Section				49 Other Ranks
	23		Brigade Reserve.	Entrenchments
	24/25		Relieved 5th Lincolns.	99 Other Ranks
	26		Strengthening trenches. Working to our Wood (inside) & Reserve Line	Strength 28/4/18
			Wiring LOISNE locality	28 Offrs O.R.
	27/28		Relieved by 1/6th Sherwood Foresters in Right sub-sector.	Bn Strength 30 874
	29		{ Improving trenches & erecting elephant shelters. Strengthening wire in front	Trench " 16 490
	30		{ During tour large quantity of salvage - including one 18 pounder gun

Arthur Hanson Capt A/L
Commdg 1/5 Bn the Sherwood Foresters

OPERATION ORDER NO. 45.   Copy No. _____

S E C R E T.   17th June, 1918.

1. A raid will be carried out on enemy's posts as follows on the night of 18th/19th June, 1918:-
    "A" Party. House at X.16.c.60.70.
    "B" Party. House at X.16.c.75.75.
    "C" Party. Post at X.16.c.73.90.
    "D" Party. Post at X.16.c.45.72.
    "E" Party. Post at X.16.c.53.90.

2. Raiding parties will be constituted as follows:-
    "A" Party   1 Officer and 25 Other Ranks from "C" Coy.
    "B" Party   1 Sergt. and 20 Other Ranks from "C" Coy.
    "C" Party   1 Officer and 25 Other Ranks from "C" Coy.
    "D" Party   A Lewis Gun Section and 1 N.C.O. and 6 Other Ranks from "D" Coy.
    "E" Party   1 Officer and 20 Other Ranks from "D" Coy

3. Standing Patrols to protect the flanks of raid will be found as follows:-
    2 Lewis Gun Sections including 4 Rifle Grenadiers from "A" Company on Right Flank about X.16.c.60.30.
    2 Lewis Gun Sections including 4 Rifle Grenadiers on Left Flank about X.16.a.05.05. from "B" Company.
    These will be in position at ZERO less 15 minutes.

4. All parties will be in assembly positions at ZERO less 30 minutes as follows:-
    "A" Party. at X.16.c.22.35.
    "C" Party at X.16.c.23.32.
    "B" Party at X.16.c.25.30.
    "D" abd "E" Parties at X.16.c.25.50.
    Right Flank Patrol at X.22.a.20.90.
    Left Flank Patrol at X.15.d.95.90.
   O.C. "A" and "B" Companies will arrange to have covering parties out in front of assembly positions from ZERO less 40 minutes until ZERO.

5. At ZERO to ZERO plus 5 our artillery barrage will be put down on area to be raided and enemy posts on flanks.
   At ZERO plus 5 artillery barrage will lift 200 yards to selected targets and all parties will advance to their objective by routes as shewn on attached map A 1 .

6. Parties "A", "B" and "D" will remain at their objectives until parties "C" and "E" have withdrawn. They will then withdraw in the following order, "B", "A" and "D".
   O.C."E" Party will inform O.C."A" Party when his men are all clear
   O.C."C" Party will inform O.C."B" Party.
   O.C."B" Party will inform O.C."A" Party.
   O.C."A" Party will inform O.C."D" Party when they are respectively withdrawing.

7. Raiders will only remain at their objectives sufficiently long to deal effectively with any enemy in the posts.

8. Any prisoners captured by "A", "B" or "D" parties will be sent in under escort to O.C.Raid H.Q. at X.22.a.10.90., immediately their objectives have been captured.
   Any prisoners captured by "C" and "E" parties will be brought back by the parties themselves. In each party special men should be detailed to cut off shoulder straps from all enemy dead for identification purposes and to show number killed.

9. O.C.Raid will be Captain Glew. His H.Q. will be at X.22.a.10.90.

continued.

A.F.25.

Report on Raid by the 1/5th Battalion, Sherwood Foresters, on the night of 18th/19th June, 1918.

1. After careful reconnaissance by day and night patrols, enemy posts were located definitely:-
    House at X.16.c.60.70.   day and night.
    House at X.16.c.75.75.   probably night only.
    Post at X.16.c.45.72.   night only.
    Post at X.16.c.53.90.   day and probably night.
    and a machine gun post infinite and approximately at X.16.c.73.90.

2. I decided to raid these posts under an artillery barrage and to destroy the two house as they were apparently being used as observation posts by the enemy.
    My plan was to attack the post from the south as reconnaissance had proved that there was no wire on this, whilst a good belt ran from the Rue De BOIS northwards in front of enemy's post.

3. Attached copy of orders gives details of parties engaged on raid.

4. Narrative.
    Artillery barrage commenced punctually at ZERO, (12-35am.) and was excellent except on right, where it fell rather short, and delayed a party of "B" party from moving forward.

    "A" Party. 2nd Lieut. Waterhouse and 25 Other Ranks reached their objective - house at X.16.c.60.70. and captured two prisoners with a British Lewis Gun adapted to German ammunition, in position near house.
    The house was then examined and one prisoner captured in cellar. House was then flooded with paraffin, taken for the purpose, and burnt down. On leaving this house the O.C.Party discovered a German hiding underneath a tub, and he shot him.

    "B" Party. Sergt. Pope and 20 Other Ranks were divided by our barrage, and only the party reached their objective at X.16.c.75.75.
    Two Germans were encountered on the way to this house, and these were killed, and papers taken from their bodies.
    This house after being searched was also destroyed, and the remainder of party joined "C" Party.

    "C" Party. 2nd Lieut. Moore and 25 Other Ranks advanced along Light Railway, and found 6 enemy in trench running alongside of railway.
    Three of these were shot and killed in the trench, one bayonetted and two attempted to run towards orchard, X.16. Central. These were both killed. An Officer with knapsack also attempted to run from post at X.16.c.73.90.
    He was shot at and dropped his pack and greatcoat. He ran for some distance and then fell apparently killed. The pack and greatcoat are sent herewith, and also papers taken from some of the killed enemy. Several others were seen running into our barrage near orchard. This party now came under heavy machine gun and rifle fire from orchard, east of the railway. This was replied to with rapid fire and O.C."E" Party having completed his task, re-inforced "C" Party, and both parties then withdrew by degrees, each in turn provided covering fire for the other.

continued.

2.

"D" Party. One Lewis Gun Section and
"E" Party. 2nd Lieut. Dench and 20 Other Ranks advanced along ditch on north side of RUE De BOIS, and under wire belt located by previous daylight patrol of 2nd Lieut. Nash. This officer was unfortunately killed whilst completing an excellent reconnaissance.
"D" Party remained at their objective, the post, on road at X.16.c.45.72. found to be unoccupied, and "E" Party advanced to their objective, enemy post at X.16.c.53.90. on enemy side of wire belt. Before advancing from road a smoke barrage was put down north of objective with No. 27 rifle grenades. This proved most effective, and quite screened this party from enemy post to the north when in assembly positions and before our barrage commenced. Very Lights were fired from this enemy post, but it was found unoccupied when our men reached it. O.C. of this party then seeing that 2nd Lieut. Moore's party ("C") was being heavily fired on at once re-inforced him.
The right and left flanks protecting patrols gave much useful assistance by engaging enemy machine guns and posts with Lewis Gun fire and Rifle Grenades.

ARTILLERY. Except for the one small instance previously referred to, our barrage was really excellent. A direct hit had apparently been obtained on enemy post at X.16.c.53.90. ("C" Party's objective).

MACHINE GUNS. Useful support was given by our machine guns, firing continuously on enemy roads, tracks, and posts.

STOKES MORTARS. Our Stokes Mortars rendered valuable assistance by firing suspected enemy machine guns and posts.

COMMUNICATION. The wire from O.C. Raid H.Q. was cut early in the operation, but communication with Battn. H.Q. was maintained by Power Buzzar. Lamp communication was not established.

ROCKETS & LIGHTS. Considerable assistance was given to the raiders by white parachute rockets and very lights being fired to the flanks of the raid, and the whole area was well lit up. Red flares were lit at a point about 500 yards in rear of our outpost line at ZERO + 20 to guide the raiders back.

ENEMY CASUALTIES. 3 prisoners captured.
1 Officer and 9 O.Ranks killed.
Other Casualties unknown.

ENEMY ACTION. It appeared as if the enemy were expecting the raid as within half a minute of our barrage opening, enemy sent up twin orange followed by twin red rockets, and their barrage came down promptly on our whole Battalion front line, and roads and all tracks were heavily shelled. Enemy appeared to have evacuated most of his posts as soon as our barrage commenced. From 3-0am. to 4-0am., the enemy retaliated heavily on LIVERPOOL LINE and LE HAMEL, causing us a few casualties.

CASUALTIES. Our total casualties in the raid are 17 men wounded (mostly slight wounds). 3 of these were wounded on the flank covering party, and 3 or 4 in assembly positions by our own barrage.

continued.

RECONNAISSANCE. Great care had been taken over this, and the information gained by our reconnoitring patrols proved to have been reliable and accurate.

I consider that great credit is due to Captain Glew, O.C.Raid, and 2nd Lieuts. Waterhouse, Moore, and Dench, and all ranks engaged in the operation for the splendid way they carried out every part of the raid according to plan. The leaders shewed good initiative and the spirit of all ranks was magnificent.

                                Sd. A.E.F.Fawcus. Lieut. Col.
                                Cdg. 1/5th Bn. Sherwood Foresters.

19/6/18.

WAR DIARY or INTELLIGENCE SUMMARY

Army Form C. 2118.

July, 1918 1/5 Nott & Derby

Hour, Date, Place	Summary of Events and Information	Remarks and References to Appendices
GORRE Section 1st	Right Sub-sector Inturning Trenches Relieved by 1/5th South Staffs & moved into Divisional Reserve	Strength of Unit 5-7-18
VAUDRICOURT WOOD 2nd 3rd 4th	Training and Interior Economy – Bathing & Disinfection of Clothes Schemes & Platoon Drill – Lecture to Company Commanders & Coy Sergt Majors & Instruction of Captains to Commanding Officer. Training under Company arrangements. Instruction by G.O.C. Division – Inspection of Army H.Q. decorated ribbons of men of No 7 platoon	Offrs O.Ranks Est. strength 39 894 Trench strength 17 544
5th	Divine Service	Casualties: Killed 2 Offrs 12 O.Ranks Wounded 2 " 25 " Wounded remained at duty 1 Offr 5 O.Rank
ESSARS Section 5th 6th 7th 8th 9th 10th 11th 12th 13th 14th 15th	Relieved 4th Leicester Regiment in Right Sub-sector Quiet tour could the exception of Artillery activity Wiring and Improving positions Relieved by 1/6th Cheshire Tunkers & moved into Brigade Reserve Artillery on both sides active – Wiring in Tunkers and Keeps Relieved by 1/5th South Staffordshire Regiment Continued	Reinforcements during month 5 Offrs 130 O.Ranks Strength of Bn 31.5.18 Offrs O.Ranks 38 935 Estd. Strength 38 935 Trench Strength 21 593

Army Form C. 2118.

WAR DIARY
or
INTELLIGENCE SUMMARY.
(Erase heading not required.)

Instructions regarding War Diaries and Intelligence Summaries are contained in F. S. Regs., Part II. and the Staff Manual respectively. Title pages will be prepared in manuscript.

Hour, Date, Place	Summary of Events and Information	Remarks and References to Appendices
VAUDRICOURT WOOD		
16th	Cleaning up - Interior Economy	
17th	Bathing and Disinfection of Clothing and Equipment - Training	
18th	Training under Company Arrangements. At night covered by two	
	Coys ESSARS [?] for digging Cable Trench in forward area. - The whole Battn. employed	
19th	Battalion Sports	19th July 1918
20th	Coys Gunners and Lot Class shot of the Lewis firing on range.	Lieut Col N. G. Tamme D.S.O. M.C.
	NCOs Drill - Remainder of Battn. digging protection trench ground trench in	proceeded to England.
	Vaudricourt Wood	Major A. Hartney M.C.
21st	Divine Service	took over Command of
ESSARS Section		Battalion
22nd		
23rd	Relieved 7th Battn. South Staffordshire Regiment in Essars sector	
24th	Quiet - Improving trenches & wiring	
25th	Enemy raid on Right Front Company successfully driven off by machine gun fire	
26th		
27th	Battery active. Sentwery trench &c	
28th	Relieved by the Sherwood Foresters & moved into Brigade Reserve	
	Working on Improvement of Trenches in Right Sub-sector	
29th		
30th	Relieved 9th Sherwood Foresters in Right Sub-sector	
31st	Quiet	

Astacllus
Major
Odg 1/5th Bn Sherwood Foresters

WAR DIARY August 1918

1/5- North'd Derby

INTELLIGENCE SUMMARY
Army Form C. 2118.

(Erase heading not required.)

Hour, Date, Place	Summary of Events and Information	Remarks and References to Appendices
ESSARS Section		
1	Right Sub-sector	London Gazette
2	Relief by Col. Roth. Sub. the Regiment and moved out. Bn. Reserve	Capt. & Major N. Harburg MC attended 116th Bgd. C.O. from
VERQUIN	Headquarters and two Companies	3rd August 1918 whilst
VAUDRICOURT WOOD	Two Companies	Commanding Battalion
3	Inspection of clothing, cleaning up, Interior economy	
4	Divine Service in VAUDRICOURT WOOD GOC Division present	Captain & Major M. Gryffiths M.C.
	Bathing at FOUQUIERES	joined this unit from
5		3rd Cheshire Regiment on
6	Training and inspection by Commanding Officer at HESDIGNEUL	7th August 1918 as
	Inspection by G.O.C. Division of HESDIGNEUL	Second in Command
7	Training of Car Kluits in Gas Chamber. - Shot Hawk March	
8	Training & lectures to Company Commanders	The 11th. Hussars Brigade
	Interior Economy - Cleaning up after bathing water	being disbanded, the
GORRE Section		Training Staff Company of
8	Relieved the Leicester Regiment in Right subsector	8 Officers & 119 Other Ranks
9, 10, 11	Hostile Patrols very active by Concentration by enemy activity	were posted and joined
12	Relieved by 1/8th. Warwick Cheshire and moved into Brigade Reserve	this unit on the 8th inst
14	Relieved by 1/4th. Lincoln Regiment and moved to ESSARS	
	Sector - Brigade General & relieved 1/4th Lincoln Staffs Regiment	

Forms/C. 2118/10.

WAR DIARY
or
INTELLIGENCE SUMMARY.
(Erase heading not required.)

August 1918 (Contd.)

Army Form C. 2118.

Instructions regarding War Diaries and Intelligence Summaries are contained in F. S. Regs., Part II. and the Staff Manual respectively. Title pages will be prepared in manuscript.

Hour, Date, Place	Summary of Events and Information	Remarks and References to Appendices
ESSARS Section		Strength 15/8/18 Offrs O.Ranks
15	Brigade Relieved	Both Strength 38 935
16	Relieved 5th Sherwood Foresters in Left Subsector	Trench Strength 31 593
16-17-18-19	Own patrols very active.	
	During this tour Enemy reinforcement on part of enemy observed	Casualties -
	and on the 18th the Bosches on left front observed, reinforcements	Killed 10 O.Ranks
	on 19th we commenced to push forward and advanced his to	Wounded 1 Officer 39 O Ranks
	Hing Street and got round the village of LE TOURET	Wounded remained at duty
	S. of the enemy together with 2 machine guns were captured	1 Officer 6 O Ranks
	Many of the enemy were killed	
	Relieved by 6th South Staffs Regt. and moved into Div Reserve	Evacuated Demarcation Area
20		4 Officers 85 O Ranks
VAUDRICOURT WOOD		
21	Bathing - Cleaning up and Interior Economy	Reinforcements
22	Invitation to Commanding Officer at HESDIGNEUL	10 Officers 45 Oth Ranks
	(written by G.O.C. Division) for that cancelled.	
23	"D" Company moves to LE QUESNOY locally	31st August 1918
24	Remained	Of disbandment N.C.I.A.C.O
	Proceeded by train from LAPIERETTE siding to KANTARA Dumps for work	forwarded to Bank
	on Line of Rlwhd N. of GORRE.	
25	Training - Rushes with No 36 Rifle Grenades.	
26	Relieved 5th Lincoln Regiment in Support Line	Strength 31/8/18 Offrs O.Ranks
GORRE SECTION		Both Strength 40 902
26	Enemy Patrols Active - Eyes slightly advanced	Trench Strength 22 513
27-28-29	Relieved by 6th Sherwood Foresters and moved into Brigade Reserve	
30		

Alfred King Lt Colonel
1/5th Sherwood Foresters

H 40

1/5 Shannon Frazier
We 42
139/46
SEPT OCT 1918

On His Majesty's Service.

Army Form C. 2118.

WAR DIARY
-OF-
INTELLIGENCE SUMMARY.
(Erase heading not required.)

September 1918 1/5 Notts Derby Vol 4

Place	Date	Hour	Summary of Events and Information	Remarks and references to Appendices
GORRE ? Section	1		Brigade Reserve Owing to enemy withdrawing Battn took over new frontline 2 Companies LIVERPOOL LINE 2 Companies NEWCASTLE LINE	Strengths 1-9-18 S. Knights 20 902 Rank & File 22 540
	4		The Battalion attacked and advanced further to took in the vicinity of RICHBOURG ST VAAST & afterwards took over trenches on OLD BRITISH FRONTLINE	Casualties Killed 2O/R 28 Ranks
	5		Owing to the advance being considerably reduced Garrison was cut over by 12th Devons on left and 5th Dragoons on right.	Wounded 3 O/R 117 Ranks Wounded Unclass 23 Ranks
	6		Battalion moved to Tuilleh nr BETHUNE - Battery & Grenery & Company works	Missing unaccounted 15 O Ranks
LAPUGNOY	7		Marched to new billeting area	Missing 1 Officer 14 O Ranks
	8		Lost march - Church Parade in rule	
	9		Tactical scheme - Afternoon Greening & Sports	Reinforcements 3 Officer 120 Ranks
	10		Interior Economy & Greenery	
	11		Greening under Company arrangement	
	12	9.28am 12.50pm	Entrained at CALONNE RICQUART Detrained at CORBIE and marched to billets LAHOUSSOYE	Strengths 30-9-18 S/m 38 Rank & File 60 500
LAHOUSSOYE	13		Rest march & Greenery	Sent in 18 & 19
	14		Tactical scheme	
	15		Divine Service	
	16		Tactical scheme - Tactical scheme for Officers under Brigade	
	17		Tactical scheme & Battery	
	18		Drill	
	19	9.30am	Entrained LAHOUSSOYE detrained POEUILLY station Greenery	

Army Form C. 2118.

WAR DIARY September 1918
INTELLIGENCE SUMMARY.
(Erase heading not required.)

Instructions regarding War Diaries and Intelligence Summaries are contained in F.S. Regs., Part II and the Staff Manual respectively. Title pages will be prepared in manuscript.

Place	Date	Hour	Summary of Events and Information	Remarks and references to Appendices
PONTRUET	20		Relieved 60th Rifles (1st K.R.R. 2nd Brigade) and Right Sector, BERTOUCOURT.	
	21		Transport and O.M. Stores moved to VENDELLES	
	22		Transport + Q.M. Stores moved to HANCOURT owing to heavy hostile shelling. Enemy attacked our trenches + effected an entry. Our own Counter Attached same day + recaptured trench together with rough 20 normandie. Our Casualties 8 killed 20 wounded	
	24		Divisional attack on PONTRUET + FORCANS front. Both attacked + captured. BEUX + LEDUC Trenches (see attached reports)	
	26		Relieved by 1st CAMERONS and took over billets at VADENCOURT	
	29		Held (North Midland) Division attacked and captured portion of ST QUENTIN Canal + HINDENBURG LINE (SEIGFRIED LINE) North of ST QUENTIN (see attached Operation Order, Report, & Maps)	
	30		Battalion Billets in the captured village (LEHAUCOURT)	

R.R. Raitt

O/c 16th Sherwood Foresters

WAR DIARY October 1918

1/5 Sherwood Foresters

Army Form C. 2118

INTELLIGENCE SUMMARY

Hour, Date, Place	Summary of Events and Information	Remarks and references to Appendices
LAHOUCOURT 1, 2, 3	In reserve to 32nd Division.	
4	Attack made by the Division (in connection with operation of ANZACS on left and FRENCH Corps on right) on the villages of RAMICOURT and MONTBREHAIN. 5th In. Division took one of the leading Bathns. (An attached Operation Order and report). Bathn. relieved 9th Infantry Brigade on line on SEQUEHART front. Bathn. relieved by 1/6th Bn. Worcestershire Regt. and went into Brigade Reserve. In HQ and 2 Companies in LEVERGIES, 2 Companies in SEQUEHART.	Commanding Officer Lt Col R Hocking. M.C. Capt (Adj) L.G Raymond awarded D.S.O. Lieut R.S Pratt M.C.
5		
6		
7	In Brigade Reserve. Reorganising.	
8, 9	Move to rear billeting area near MERICOURT.	
10		
MERICOURT AREA 11, 12	Cleaning up. Reorganising & Training. Move to new billeting area Bathn HQ FRESNOY – BOHAIN Road. Companies in bivouacs near JONCOURT FARM	
13	Lewis Gun Course – Training – Interior Economy. Move to billets in BOHAIN.	
BOHAIN 14–15–16	Specialists classes – Drill – Improvement of billets	

Shed 2

WAR DIARY
—or—
INTELLIGENCE SUMMARY.
(Erase heading not required.)

Army Form C. 2118.

October 1918

Instructions regarding War Diaries and Intelligence Summaries are contained in F. S. Regs., Part II. and the Staff Manual respectively. Title pages will be prepared in manuscript.

Hour, Date, Place	Summary of Events and Information	Remarks and references to Appendices
17	Attack made to Denison near REGNICOURT. 2 Companies attached to 8th Sherwood Foresters in attack. Both Reorganisation and 2 Companies in Reserve. (On attached situation order and report). Relieved by 6th Bn Sherwood Foresters at night and moved into Brigade Reserve.	Strength 1-10-18. Offr OR. Bath. Strength 38 801 Trench Strength 21 450 Casualties Killed 2 Officers 31 O Ranks Wounded 10 Officers 182 O Ranks Wounded - Remained at duty 4 O Ranks Prisoners 20 O Ranks (sick) Evac. Dis. Area 6 Officers 111 Other Ranks Reinforcements 11 Officers 310 Other Ranks Strength 31.10.18 Bath. Strength 39 Offs 765 OR Trench do 23 . 512
18	Division out of Line and moved back to FRESNOY LE GRAND. Baths billeted in sugar factory.	
FRESNOY LE GRAND		
19	Bathing - Cleaning up and Indoor Economy.	
20	Divisional Church Service - GOC Division attended service.	
21, 22, 23	Drill - Training - Specialist Classes.	
24	Route march.	
25	Demonstration in Guard Mounting - Bathing.	
	New by Divisional Band. Demonstration Return for All Officers of Battalion.	
26	Divisional Ceremonial parade - Distribution of the French Croix de Guerre by General Officer Commanding 126th. French Divsonl.	
27	Divine Service.	
28	Specialist Classes - Training.	

Sheet No 3

WAR DIARY
INTELLIGENCE SUMMARY

October 1918.

Army Form C. 2118.

Hour, Date, Place	Summary of Events and Information	Remarks and references to Appendices
BOHAIN 29	Specialists Classes - Training	
30.	Moved to new Billeting area at BOHAIN.	
31.	Specialists Classes. Drill. Intermovement of Ricub.	
	Attached Operation Orders 78 - 84 A	
	Map showing BEAUREVOIR attack 29/9/18.	
	6 Aerial Photographs do	
	4 Enamels do	

E.O. Stewart Lt/Col
Comdt. 1/5 Batln. The Seaforth Highlanders

Operation Order by 7? Coy to

SECRET   3rd October 1918

1. Information
Information as to the situation on the Somme on L?
and the French Army on the right. the 46th Division
are attacking and capturing lines from B.10.a.SE.30
to I.14.y.x. (including MONTBREHAIN)

2. Instructions
a. The Bn will line up on a line from H15.c.25.30
to H.22.a.85.70. 2 Platoons in front one in close
support. at ZERO will advance and capture
the red line from H.6.b.45.00 to I.y.a.be.x

b. Disposition
        B company on Left.   C Company on Right.
        A Coy Left Sect.   D Coy Right sect
        C & D Coys at H.15.c.95.40.

c. Order of march will be - B D C A Coys HQ D details,
Companies will move by platoons at 15 yards interval
as far as H.15.c.90.40 and then deploy to fighting order
point
Deployment will be on bearing of 157 magnetic from
Cross Roads at H.15.c.95.40. & advance on bearing
of 67 magnetic

d. Report centre will be at Bn HQ H.15.c.95.40.
e. French Mortar Section will be attached to each
forward company
f. Artillery arrangements explained personally
g. On taking objective AB will be at H.22.d.30.30.
h. ZERO will be 0600.
i. Echelon A will be brought up ready to move
Aid Post will be established at Bn HQ

                            Sd John B Raymond
                                 Captain Adjt
                            H/Lt Sherwood Forester

SECRET   Copy 8
    1/5th Bn. Sherwood Foresters
                                          5-10-18

         OPERATION ORDER No 79

1. The Battalion will relieve the 97th Inf
    Brigade in the Line tonight 5/6th Oct
    and will take over the Front from H30 d 05
    to I 19c 02
    Dispositions will be as follows:-
    A. Coy will be in Front Line
    D "   in Dug-outs at H 30 a 6.1
    C "   in Cellars at Farm at H 30 a 2.3
    B "   in Sunken Road in H 29a
    A. D & C Coys relieve the 5th Border Regt.
    and B Coy take over from the 10th Argylls
    The 139 T.M.B. will dispose 1 Section with
    Front Line Company, and Section Officer will
    live with O.C. A Coy.
    Battalion H.Q. will be at H 28 c 6.0
2. The Battn will move off in the following
    order commencing at 7-0 P.M.
    'A' 'D' 'C' 'B' & H.Q. Details. 50 yards interval
    between Platoons.

2.

Lewis Guns will be carried.
O.C. D Coy will detail 1 Platoon to be at the disposal of O C T M Section. And all arrangements will be made by O.C. D. Coy and the T M Officer concerned.

3 Further instructions will be issued with regard to rations and Cooking arrangements.

4 Lists of Stores taken over, Aeroplane Photo's & maps, dispositions etc will be forwarded to B O R with early morning reports on 8th inst.

5 Completion of Relief will be reported to B.O.R. by Runner.

6 Acknowledge.

Issued at 4-30 P.M.   2/Lieut & A/Adjt
Copy 1 - 5 Coys & H.Q.   1/5th Bn Sherwood Foresters
       6 Q M & T O.
       7 File
       8 War Diary

SECRET   139. Infantry Brigade Order. 211.

Date. 5.10.18

1. The 139. Inf. Bde. will take over the SEQUEHART front from the 14th & 97th Inf. Brigades on night 5/6th October.

(a) The 8th Battn S.F. will take over the front held by the 14th Inf. Brigade. i.e, from H.36.c.6.2 to H.30.d.0.5. This is at present held by 3 weak Battalions. The Dorsets on right, the H.L.I. in centre and the Royal-Scots on left; each of these battalion Sectors will be taken over with one company 8th S.F, the 4th Coy will be in Battalion Reserve in a position to be decided by O.C. 8th Sherwood Foresters.

(b) The 5th Battn. S.F. will take over the front held by the 97th Inf. Brigade i.e, from H.30.d.0.5 to I.19.c.0.2 with one Company in front line, one Company in dug-outs at H.30.a.6.1. one Company in Cellars at farm H.30.a.2.3. & one Company in Sunken Road in H.29.a. The first 3 companies mentioned take over from the 5th Border Regt. & the last company from the 10th Argylls.

(c) The 6th S.F. will be in Brigade Reserve & remain in present area. East of LEHAUCOURT.

(d) The 139.T.M.B. will dispose one Section with each front line Battn. Section Officer to live with a front line Company – Commander. If possible Sunken Roads approaching SEQUEHART will be covered by T.M's

(e) The 2nd Life Guards M.G. Battⁿ will cover the Brigade front strongly with M.Gs, care being taken to cover the valley approaches East of SEQUEHART.

(f) The 9th Corps Cyclists on relief by another Brigade, will come under order of G.O.C. 139. Inf. Brigade & will be in Bde Reserve taking over dug-outs in Eastern portion of LEVERGIES at present occupied by 2 Coy's of the 10th Argylls.

2. Arrangements for relief will be made between C.O's concerned, & will commence at dusk.

3. Brigade Headquarters will remain at Magny-la-Fosse H.25.a.1.1.

4. Command of Sectors will pass to G.O.C. 139. Inf. Brigade on completion of ~~relief~~ front line relief - 14th Inf. Brigade. Brigade Advanced H.Qs H.31.a.7.6. will be used as visual signalling station.

5. Reliefs will be wired to Brigade H.Qrs using the code word "RATS".

6. Acknowledge.

Captain.
Brigade Major.
139. Infantry Brigade.

Officer Commanding:-
  5th. 6th. 8th. Sherwood Foresters.
  139. T.M.B. Brigade Signals.

Notes issued in connection with relief of 14th & 97th Infantry Brigades to-night:-

1. 8th Battn S.F. H.Q will be H.33.d.2.7. at present occupied by H.L.I.

"D" Coy 2nd Life Guards M.G. Battn will have H.Qs at H.33.a.2.8. at present occupied by Royal Scots.

5th Battn S.F. will have H.Qs at H.28.c.6.0. at present occupied by Border Regt.

9th Corps Cyclists will have H.Q at H.34.a.1.9. at present occupied by by ARGYLLS.

"B" Coy 2nd Life Guards M.G. Battn will cover the 5th Bn S.F. & D Coy the 8th SF.

H.Qs of Dorset Regt is at H.33.a.3.2.

　　　　　　　　　　　　　　　[signature]
　　　　　　　　　　　　　　　Captain -
　　　　　　　　　　　　　　Brigade Major.
5.10.18　　　　　　　　　　139. Infantry Brigade

copy to 14th & 97 Battns.

Secret   Copy No 2

1/5 Sherwood Foresters OPERATION ORDER No 80

Ref. Map THORIGNY   7·10·18.

1. The 1st Bn Monmouthshire Reg't will take over the 139th Brigade Front in the SEQUEHART Sector to-night, from Southern Brigade Boundary, up to H 30.b.70.50. the 6th Div'n extending their frontage Southwards to that point.

2. Two Platoons of 1st. Monmouths will relieve the Two Platoons of "A" Coy at Quarry in H 30.d, and Sunken Road H 30.d 40.90. Two Platoons of the 1st. Bn. West Yorks will relieve 2 Platoons of A Coy in the area H 30.b.40.50. to H 30.b.0.9. One Guide per Platoon will be at Bn Hdqrs at 6·30 p.m.   On completion of relief "A" Coy will move into cellars in LEVERGIES. Guides will meet Platoons at Bn Hdqrs. Tools, S.A.A. and Bombs will be handed over to incoming Units.

2

Bnltdgis, B, C + D Coys will remain as at present.

Completion of movement will be reported by O.C. A Coy in person.

                         [signature]
                         2nd Lt & A/Adjt
                         1/5 Sherwood Foresters

Issued at 3.0 pm to:-
    Copy No 1-5   Coys and HQ
                6   Q.M + TO
                7   File
                8   War Diary

Secret.   Copy No
1/5 Sherwood Foresters Operation Order No 81
                                              8-10-18

1. The following inter Company relief
will take place tonight 8th inst.
'B' Coy will relieve 'C' Coy in the
latter Company's positions in
shell holes in H.29.b.
Company Hdqrs at H.30.a.20.35
'C' Coy will, on relief, move into
billets vacated by 'B' Coy in
LEVERGIES.
Guides for both Companies
will be met at Bn Hdqrs.

2. Completion of relief will be
reported by OC 'C' Coy in person
to Bn Hdqrs.
                          C. H. S. KIRK.
                          2nd Lieut A/Adj
                          1/5 Sherwood Foresters

Issued to:-

    'B' 'C' 'D' Coys & Q.M.

SECRET   Date 8th Oct

139th Infantry Brigade Order 203.

1. The 139 Inf. Bde & 1st MONMOUTHS will be concentrated about LEVERGIES by 7.30 am 9th Inst.
   (a) The 5th S.F. will remain in present positions.
   (b) The 6th Bn. S.F will move to area South of LEVERGIES – SEQUEHART RD. about H.33. & 34.
   (c) The 8th Bn. S.F. will move to area North of LEVERGIES – SEQUEHART RD. about H.27. & 28.
   (d) The 1st MONMOUTHS will remain at SEQUEHART.
   (e) The 139.T.M.B will move to LEVERGIES.
   Note: All above moves will be completed by 7.30 am.

2. Brigade transport will move to valley in about N.2. and 3 and H.33. Move to be completed by 11 am, B.T.O. will allot sites, Brigade Wing will move with Transport.
   454 Coy A.S.C. will be assembled about LEHAUCOURT by 1 pm.

3. Any packs or surplus stores in forward area will be dumped at Church LEHAUCOURT. (4) Brigade H.Q will close at MAGNY. la. Fosse at 10.30 pm 9th Inst, and re-open at Church LEVERGIES at the same hour.

5. Units will forward to Bde. H.Q by 9.30 am exact location of their H.Q. & Troops.

6. Guides will meet supply waggons at LEHAUCOURT Church at 1300 9th Inst.

7. Acknowledge.

8.10.18.

Captain
Brigade Major - 139.Inf. Bde

Operation Order 82
Secret   10/10/18

The Bn will move tonight to MERICOURT
Order of march HQ A C B D Coys
Parade outside Coy Billets ready
to move off from LEVERGIES
at 5.15 hrs. Companies at
100 yards interval. B & D Coys
will join column as it passes
SEQUEHART
Dress Fighting Order
Packs & surplus stores will be moved
dumped at QM Stores
Coy Limbers will move with Coys
Mess Cart & maltese cart in rear
of Bn
Remainder of Transport will move
under Bde arrangements
2 Battle Details will move with Transport
3 Values in LEVERGIES will be
dumped at QM Stores at once
Stores at SEQUEHART will be
left under a guards to be found
by B Coy at X Roads H 30 c 10.70
& these will be picked up by
baggage wagons

                                Lewis M/Kay
15th Sherwood Foresters

SECRET

139 Inf Bde Order No. 214

10/10/18

1. The Bde Group will be formed at once & will concentrate about MERICOURT and BEAUREGARD. The Staff Capt will allot areas.

2. Units will move independently as under:—
   - 139 T.M.B. to be clear of LEVERGIES by 16.50 hrs
   - 6th S. Fors " " " " " " 17.00 hrs
   - 8th S. Fors " " " " " " 17.15 hrs
   - 5th S. Fors " " " " " " 17.30 hrs
   - 465 Fd Coy R.E. to move after 17.30 hrs
   - 'A' Coy M G Battn will move after 17.30 hrs

3. Packs & Surplus stores will be dumped at present Q.M. Stores.

4. Coy Limbers will move with Bns, remainder of transport will move under arrangements to be made by B.T.O; not to leave present lines before 5.45pm.

5. Bde HQ will close at LEVERGIES at 17 hours today & reopen at FRESNOY at the same hour.

6. Acknowledge.

R.V. Whitmore Capt
Bde Cb a/or 139 I Bde

Issued at 16.10 hrs.

1/5th. Bn. Sherwood Foresters.

Operation Order No. 83.

SECRET.

Copy No.

12th. October, 1918.

Reference Map 62.B.

The Battalion will move to New Billeting res to-day as follows:-
Headquarters to House J.7.b.
"A" Coy.   J.1.a.
"B" "   J.1.c.
"C" "   I.6.b.
"D" "   I.6.c. & d.

Parade in Column of Route on Track I.15.d. at 3-15.p.m. in the following orders-

H.Q.s.; "A"; "B" "C"; "D" Coys.
Coys. will move at 100 yds. interval. Route will be BE UREGARD track I.16. c. & d. — FRESNOY — BILLETING AREA.
Lewis Gun Limbers and Cookers will proceed with Coys; Water Carts, Mess Cart and Medical Cart in rear of Battalion.
Tents and Trench Shelters will be struck immediately and stacked on side of track at I.15.d.80.30. together with Officers Baggage, this will be conveyed to new Billeting res under arrangements to be made by the R.Q.M.S.
Provost Corpl. will arrange to take charge of all stores until necessary limbers arrive.

(Sg.)   E.H. Kirkby.   2/Lieut. & A/Adjt.
1/5th. Bn. The Sherwood Foresters.

To:-
All Companies.

Reference Operation Order No. 84.

"Z" Day is the 17th October, 1918.

ZERO Hour will be 0520 hours.

Companies will leave present billets as follows:-

```
       Headquarters.-    0120
A     "A" Company.       0130
D     "D" Company.       0140
B     "B" Company.       0150
C     "C" Company.       0200
```

Care will be taken that the traffic on the
NORAIN - VAUX ANDIGNY Road is interfered with
as little as possible.

        Sd. C.H.Kirkby, 2/Lt. & A/Adjt.
    1/5th Bn. The Sherwood Foresters.

14th October, 1918.

SECRET.

Reference Operation Order No. 84.

Reference para. 3 Special Instructions, sub-para. (c) and para. 7 Barrage.

The Protective Barrage will rest for 10 minutes South of BOHAIN - ARDIGNY Les FERMES Road and not 30 minutes as stated.

After 10 minutes it will lift to S.O.S. Line where it will remain for 20 minutes.

In consequence, "C" Company will be able to push forward and consolidate their position 20 minutes earlier than stated, i.e. at ZERO plus 103 minutes.

                      Sd. E.H.Kirkby, 2nd Lieut. & A/Adjt.
      1/5th Bn. The Sherwood Foresters.

16th October, 1918.

OPERATION ORDER No. 84.   Copy No. _____

S E C R E T.   16th October, 1918.

Reference Map:- 62 b. N.E. Edition 3 a Local.

1. At ZERO hour on "Z" Day the 46th Division will capture and consolidate the Line of BOHAIN to ARDIGNY Les FERMES Road within the Divisional Boundary, the 139th Brigade on Right and 138th Brigade on Left, the 137th Brigade remaining in its present position.
It is expected the FRENCH will attack South of FORET d'ANDIGNY.
The 8th Sherwood Foresters plus two companies 5th Sherwood Foresters will carry out the attack on the 139 Brigade Front with the 5th Sherwood Foresters less two companies in support and the 6th Sherwood Foresters in reserve.

2. Forming Up.
At ZERO - 60 minutes "B" Company will be formed up on a two platoon frontage in rear of the centre company 8th Sherwood Foresters.
"C" Company on a two platoon frontage in rear of the right company 8th Sherwood Foresters, immediately south of the BOHAIN - VAUX AUDIGNY Road in D.6.c and d.
Battalion Headquarters and Details, "A" and "D" Companies along the edge of the wood in D.12.d. These will dig in.
Companies will report to B.H.Q. when they are formed up.

3. Special Instructions.
(a) "B" Company will follow in rear of centre Company of 8th Sherwood Foresters and will mop up the clearings in E.7.d., E.8.c. and E.13.b., and will then assist in mopping up REGNICOURT. On completion of this it will withdraw to high ground E.7.d. and E.13.b., and take up fire positions. This company will come under the orders of O.C. 8th Sherwood Foresters, for immediate counter attack should our line be penetrated.
(b) "C" Company will follow in rear of the right front company, 8th Sherwood Foresters.
On the protective barrage lifting at ZERO plus 123 minutes it will push forward and
  (i) with one platoon attack the small copse, E.14.c. and consolidate on the Southern side.
  (ii) with two platoons capture and consolidate the trench line in E.13.d. as far south as E.13.d.70.10.
On completion of this 5 sections will face West into the RIQUERVAL Wood and 3 sections will face South towards HENNECHIES Wood.

4. Machine Guns.
1 Section (Lt. Lorimer) "A" Company 46th M.G. Battalion will move with left platoon "C" Company, and assist in consolidating copse E.14.c.

5. Trench Mortars.
One Section under 8th Sherwood Foresters will be at about E.7.d.70.10. and will be available to assist two right platoons "C" Company if required.

6. Tanks.
One tank (No. 9146) will follow "C" Company and assist in clearing trench E.13.d.

7. Barrage.
The barrage will remain on the opening line for 9 minutes and then advance at the rate of 100 yards in three minutes. On reaching line approximately 300 yards South of BOHAIN and ARDIGNY Les FERMES Road, barrage will rest 30 minutes and then cease. One round smoke shells will be fired at each lift.

P. T. O.

Operation order continued.

8. <u>Headquarters.</u>
Advanced Brigade Headquarters will be at D.11.d.20.90.
From ZERO to ZERO plus 2 hours, the Battalion Headquarters will be at house D.6.c.50.30. and will then move to D.12.d.25.30.

9. <u>Aid Post.</u> Aid Post will be at house D.6.c.50.30.
<u>Bearers Posts.</u> will be established by 46th Divisional Field Artillery along BOHAIN - VAUX AUDIGNY Road, and BOHAIN - ARDIGNY Les FERMES Road.

10. <u>Synchronising.</u>
Signalling Officer will synchronise watches at Advanced Brigade at ZERO minus 3 hours.
"B" and "C" Companies will synchronise at Battalion H.Q. at ZERO minus 90 minutes.

11. Acknowledge.

                                            2nd Lieut. & A/Adjutant.
                             1/5th Bn. The Sherwood Foresters.

Copies issued at 5-0pm. to:-

Copies 1 to 4.	"A", "B", "C", "D" Companies.
5.	Brigade Headquarters.
6.	8th Sherwood Foresters.
7.	6th Sherwood Foresters.
8.	Commanding Officer.
9.	2nd in Command.
10.	War Diary.
11.	H.Q. Details.

Operation Orders No. 94.A   Copy No. 8.

SECRET.   20th. October, 1918.

Reference Map 51.b. Scale 1/40,000.

1. The Battalion will move into DORAIN Area today taking over billets vacated by the 8/8th. Battn. Royal Scots.

2. The Battalion will parade in Full Marching Order on Ground opposite Factory at 13.45 ready to move off.
   Order of March:-
       Headquarters, "A" "B" "C" "D" Coy.
   100 yds. Interval will be maintained between Companies.
   Lewis Gun Limbers and Cookers will be in rear of Companies.
   Medical Cart and Maltese Cart in rear of Battalion.

3. Blankets rolled in bundles of ten tied and labelled, Officers Mess Kit, Officers Valises, Orderly Room and Pioneer Boxes will be dumped outside B.O.R. at 12.30.

4. All Water Bottles will be filled from Water Cart prior to moving off.

5. Billets will be left in a clean and sanitary condition and a certificate to this effect rendered to B.O.R.

6. Guides will meet the Battalion at M.21.c.95.00.

                                                    C.N.Kirkby
                                                    Capt. & Adjt.
                                                    1/8th. Bn. Sherwood Foresters.

Copies issued at 11.00. to:-
   Copies 1 to 4. "A" "B" "C" "D" Coys.
          5. Commanding Officer.
          6. Headquarters Details.
          7. Medical Officer.
          ✓8. War Diary.
          9. File.
         10. Q.M. & T.O.

WAR DIARY
INTELLIGENCE SUMMARY

November 1918 1/5 N'th Derby

Army Form C. 2118

Hour, Date, Place	Summary of Events and Information	Remarks and References to Appendices
		1/5 Strengths 1-11-18
		Before O.R.
		En Strength 39 785
		Trench Strength 23 513
		Casualties
		Wounded Officers NIL Other Ranks 7
		Killed Officers — Other Ranks 1
		Evacuated (Personnel) hrs 45
		Reinforcements Officers 10 Other Ranks 206
BOHAIN		
1.	Training — Company and Specialists	
2.	Bathing and Training	
3.	Divine Service — Moved to ESCAUFOURT.	
4.	Bath on recent — Advanced on CATILLON and billeted there	
5.	Moved to LAGROIX — enemy still retiring. Both moved on to ERRVART where billetted. — Enemy delaying rather heavily	
6.	Relieved 6th Notts Derwent Forden in front and advanced through PRISCHES where 5 Germans, 2 Trench Mortars + 5 Machine guns were captured. (PRISCHES being rather heavily shelled) and moved forward to CARTIGNIES.	
7.	Front line taken over by 135th Brigade which continued to follow the enemy	
8.	Proceeded to new area — LE GRAND FAYT + billeted	
10.	Moved to CARTIGNIES — Cleaning up.	
11.	Medal Presentation by G.O.C. Division	
12.	Moved to new billets at BOULOGNE.	
13.	Interior Economy. Information received that Hostilities had ceased	
14.	Moved to new billets in LANDRECIES	
LANDRECIES		
15.	Training — Company + Specialists	
16.	Bathing + Training	
17.	Divine Service. — (Divisional parade (service) and Medal Presentation by G.O.C. Division	

Army Form C. 2118.

WAR DIARY November 1918
INTELLIGENCE SUMMARY.
(Erase heading not required.)

Instructions regarding War Diaries and Intelligence Summaries are contained in F. S. Regs., Part II. and the Staff Manual respectively. Title pages will be prepared in manuscript.

Hour, Date, Place	Summary of Events and Information	Remarks and References to Appendices
LANDRECIES 18 to 30	Route March. The Battn employed in advancing all War Material and generally cleaning up of the Battle Field.	Strength 29-11-18 Offrs. 8R En Strength 35 848 Present Strength 22 656
29	Hd. were employed as Minors in Coal Pits & detachdes to Base for transfer to England to again take up Coal Employment.	

M.L Futt Lieut Col
C/g 1/5th Bn. The Sherwood Foresters

Photographs Extracted from this diary
JCB
19/11/25

"A" FORM
MESSAGES AND SIGNALS

Prefix	Code	Words	Charge	This message is on a/c of:	Recd. at ... m
Office of Origin and Service Instructions		Sent			Date
		At		Service	From
		To			
		By		(Signature of "Franking Officer.")	By

TO: Headquarters, 139th Infantry Brigade

Sender's Number	Day of Month	In reply to Number	
*H 2	4		AAA

Ref your 314/157/G of 3rd inst
Name of NCO for Course
97463 L/c W Hughes

I do not require Officer vacancy for this Course.

From: 5 Battn Sherwood Foresters
Place:
Time:

The above may be forwarded as now corrected. (Z)

Censor. Signature of Addresser or person authorised to telegraph in his name.
* This line should be erased if not required.

WAR DIARY December, 1918.

INTELLIGENCE SUMMARY. 1/5 N & Derby

Army Form C. 2118.

Hour, Date, Place	Summary of Events and Information	Remarks and References to Appendices
LANDRECIES		Battalion Strength 1-12-18
		Officers / O.Ranks
	His Majesty the King passed through the Town and was cheered and heartily both by the French Civil Population and the British Troops.	Total Strength 35 / 656 available for work 23
1st.		Evacuated Personnel Sick 1 Officer / 20 Other Ranks
	During the month of December the Battalion had been engaged in generally cleaning up the Battle field in the vicinity of the town of LANDRECIES, and collecting all War Materials to a central dump formed by the Division.	No. of men despatched to England for Civil Employment during month
		Miners 239
		Postal Men 4
		Reinforcements 4 Officers / 41 O.Ranks
		Battalion Strength 31-12-18
		Officers / O.Ranks
		Total Strength 34 / 673 available for work 24 / 482
	C.N.Buckle Lt Col Comdg 1/5 Bn	
	Capt 1/5th Bn The Sherwood Foresters	

F.F.

Army Form C. 2118.

WAR DIARY
or
INTELLIGENCE SUMMARY.

January 1919 1/5 N. Derby

Hour, Date, Place	Summary of Events and Information	Remarks and References to Appendices
LANDRECIES 1st to 11th	Battalion engaged in clearing the Battle field of all War Material, and filling in Trenches, Craters & Shell holes in the vicinity of LANDRECIES.	W/Strength Strength 3/1/19 Officers O.Ranks Total 38 692 Working 24 482
	Moved to new area	Lt Col R.J. Ball M.C. left for demobilization 3/1/19 Lt Col M.J. Amey DSO (North Staffordshire Regiment) joined Battn in command of Officer 6/1/19
BEAUREPAIRE 12th to 31st	Battalion engaged in clearing the Battle field of all War Material, and filling in Trenches, Craters & Shell holes in the vicinity of BEAUREPAIRE	Reinforcements 42 Other Ranks
	Manouvres of each day docketed to above.	Casualties during month Officers Other Ranks — 2 134
	Total Demobilized during month W.O.'s Lce/Cpl — 1 Acting 95th Sherwood Foresters	Strength 31/1/19 Officers O.Ranks Total 37 369 Working 25 293

WAR DIARY
INTELLIGENCE SUMMARY.

Army Form C. 2118.

February 1919

Hour, Date, Place	Summary of Events and Information	Remarks and references to Appendices
BEAUREPAIRE 1st to 18th	Battalion engaged in clearing the Battle field of all War Material, and filling in Trenches, Craters, & Shell Holes in the vicinity of BEAUREPAIRE	Batt. Strength 1-2-19 Offrs O/Ranks Total 34 564 Working 25 343 Lieut Col. R.A. Abney D.S.O. left and to take over command of Yorkshire Staffs Regt & Major T. Chetwott D.S.O. T.D. took over Command of Battalion 25/7/19 Demobilized during the month Offrs 4 O/Ranks 762 Reinforcements Nil Evacuated to hospital Base 11 O/Rks Batt. Strength 28-2-19 Offrs O/Ranks Total 29 288 Working 20 201
CATILLON 19th	Battalion shayed one night without moving to next billeting area	
BETHENCOURT 20th to 28th	Battalion engaged in clearing the Battle field of all War Material, and filling in Trenches &c in the vicinity of BETHENCOURT A good part of the time during the month has been devoted to Sport.	

M Curry Major
Cdg 1/5th Sherwood Foresters

WAR DIARY March 1919.
INTELLIGENCE SUMMARY.
(Erase heading not required.)

Army Form C. 2118.

Appl 47

Hour, Date, Place	Summary of Events and Information	Remarks and references to Appendices
BETHENCOURT.		Batt. Strength 1-3-19
1st to 31st.	Battalion engaged in clearing the battle field of all War Material and filling in trenches &c in the vicinity of BETHENCOURT.	Officers O.Rs Total 29 288 Working 20 201 Demobilized during month Officers Other Ranks 9 30 Evacuated Sick from 6 Posted to 535 Bath H.D.y Bn 6 Officers Joined from 139 *Bath R.aily* 8 Other Ranks Batt. Strength 28/3/19 Officers O.Rs 1/13 261 Total 5 156 Working
	A good deal of time during the month has been devoted to sport.	

Martin
Lieut Col
O/c 15th Sherwood Foresters

Army Form C. 2118.

WAR DIARY
or
INTELLIGENCE SUMMARY.
(Erase heading not required.)

April 1919 1/5th N[otts] Derby

Hour, Date, Place	Summary of Events and Information	Remarks and References to Appendices

BETHENCOURT

1st to 14th — Salvaging War Material in the vicinity of BETHENCOURT

15th to 30th — On Orders having to form Drumers at War Companies on 15th inst. Battalion was practically reduced to Cadre Establishment and time has been devoted to clearing up, and keeping on a serviceable condition, Battalion Equipment.

D. Newstead Lieut. Col.
O/c 1/5th Sherwood Foresters

Army Form C. 2118.

WAR DIARY
or
INTELLIGENCE SUMMARY.
(Erase heading not required.)

May 1919. 1/5 N'y Derby

9.68. H.9

Hour, Date, Place	Summary of Events and Information	Remarks and references to Appendices
BETHENCOURT		Total Strength 2.5.19 3 Rander
		Offrs 59 39
		Other Strength 9 14 39
1st to 31st	The Battalion having been practically reduced to Cadre Establishment remained at BETHENCOURT awaiting orders	Examined Dorches N4
		Demobilized during 9. O'Ranks 2504
		month
		Transfers to
		Reserve y Officers Corp 1
		Total Strength 31/5/19 Offr/o'Ranks 37
		Offrs 9 28
		Other Strength 4
		Working Strength

D. Nestal
Lieut Col
Comg 1/5 Sherwood Foresters

www.ingramcontent.com/pod-product-compliance
Lightning Source LLC
Chambersburg PA
CBHW081529160426
43191CB00011B/1720